A
MILITARY
MEMSAHIB

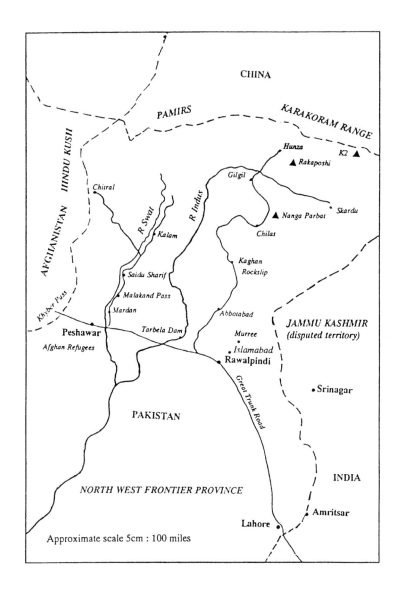

A sketch map of north-western Pakistan

A

MILITARY

MEMSAHIB

The lighthearted impressions
of a Defence Attache's Wife
Islamabad • Pakistan
1982 - 1985

Rosemary Watts

Published by Owl Press, P.O. Box 315 Downton, Salisbury, Wiltshire. SP5 3YE. 1994

Printed in the UK by Intype

British Library Cataloguing - in - Publication data. A catalogue record for this book is available from the British Library.

Publisher's ISBN: 1 898052 35 2

Foreword

Rosemary and Colin Watts arrived in Islamabad in exciting times. The Russians had invaded and occupied Afghanistan and a guerilla war was raging across Pakistan's western border. On the eastern front was an un-friendly , and in Pakistan's eyes a menacing ,India with whom three wars had already been fought. Internally Pakistan was governed by a militray dictatorship. All this was quite enough to be going on with to keep the British Defence Attache busy, while performing the leisurely and stately minuet of diplomatic life which carried on regardless of the wars and crises of the real world outside.

Rosemary observes the scene with sardonic amusement and understand-ing. It is people and their oddities that she describes and not politics. In this she stands with the great Victorian memsahibs who over the years wrote about their lives in India. Indeed the life she describes would still in many respects be recognisable to her Victorian predecessors.

Her picture of Pakistan is unsentimental and does not attempt to hide the warts but behind the frustration , occassional irritation and the clashes with petty bureaucracy lies an obvious sympathy and affection particularly for the ordinary man and woman struggling to make a living against consid-erable odds. The pride and natural friendliness of the Pakistan people shines through.

There are echoes of the often maligned Kipling here. She has Kipling's eye for detail and the ability to make a scene come alive. Life in the Diplo-matic Corps in Islamabad and travelling in Pakistan really was as she describes it, with its mixture of the trivial and the sublime, of tragedy, comedy and farce. Diplomats have a tendency to see it all as sublime and it is good for their sense of proportion to see themselves and their life through the eyes of a non diplomatic military memsahib.

Oliver Forster

Sir Oliver Forster
British Ambassador, Pakistan 1979-1984

For my husband Colin
who made it all possible,
and for our children
Caroline, Andrew, Nigel and Kay
and their families.

A Military Memsahib

Dawn was breaking. A rosy glow tinged the silver wings and illuminated the engines that had brought us through the night and were now heading us towards the sunrise. Far to the south were the warm waters of the Arabian Sea. The early morning mist shrouded the far distant peaks as yet unseen. The soft blues, pinks and greys of the morning twilight gave way to primrose and yellow as the bright face of the sun beamed up over the horizon. Gradually, as the mist cleared, we could discern our first glimpse of the landscape below. The rays of the sun brought out into sharp relief the dry rocky escarpments, the barren ravines ridges and deserts below. The early morning light gave the earth a chocolate coloured hue with coffee marbling. Here and there huge furrows had been gouged out of rock as if with a giant cats paw. We could see swirls and eddies of rock that perhaps once melted, had hardened and set into vast jagged teeth.

Far below we could see the sprawling muddy rivers, the thread of tiny roads and the first signs of habitation. The land looked bare of vegetation. Who were the people who lived down there? What did they do? How did they live? What will they make of us from the other side of the earth? We of different colour, customs, conventions and clothes? They had seen the likes of us before. Our forefathers had had roots there and had helped to shape their destinies. They had become so accustomed to and had such affection for the people and country that they chose to end their days there. As we sped northwards we had time to muse on the winds of fortune that had blown us in the direction of the subcontinent of India and to Pakistan in particular.

Those military forefathers of ours, and Colin's father was among them, could expect to spend many years overseas during their service. Those were the days when the British Empire was spread around the world. It was to this part of the country that Colin's father came in 1923. A young Signals Officer, it presented to him opportunity for travel, sport, adventure and the extra cash that serving in India as it was then would bring. Colin's father Captain John Athelwold Iremonger (Cubby) Watts served in the North-West Frontier Province, Quetta, Calcutta and Central India, Murree, Mhow and finally at Ranchi.

When Colin was at school in England the news came through that his mother had been taken ill, eating what they guessed was an unwashed tomato. It was cholera. Racking pains and fever hastened the dreaded disease and the dehydration process against which there was no cure in those days. Within twelve hours she was dead. Twelve hours later she was buried in the cemetery at Ranchi. Heartbroken, Colin's father returned to England, never to return to India again. None of the family had ever visited her grave. Colin's posting to Pakistan was to give us that opportunity.

Memories of those times will fade with the old soldiers who served there. It will be left to us to find out what we can about them from museums and libraries, or from the old photographs, cuttings and letters bundled together now gathering dust in loft and attic.

Nowadays the prospects of serving overseas become ever more limited. Though opportunities of a different sort abound for the young soldiers. Adventure training, orienteering, canoeing, trekking, skiing, sailing, round the world, yachting, potholing and mountaineering, would be enough to try the stout-hearted, the brave and the adventurous.

It seemed a very appropriate end to Colin's service in the Army when he was asked to become the Defence Attache to the British Embassy in Islamabad, Pakistan. Here seemed a perfect opportunity to revisit those places seen as a boy, heard of as a young man, and read about in the Army.

I had no first hand experience of India or Pakistan. I could only conjure up visions of pictures seen in dusty albums of King George 5th and Queen Mary, of Durbars, of Viceroys and Maharajas, of pikes and pennants, pith helmets and puggarees, turbans and tight trousers. I remembered groups of turbaned and bewhiskered old gentlemen in khaki uniforms in khaki coloured photographs portraying the stiff upper lip in some beleaguered outpost in the mountains. I thought of elephants, tigers and snakes, also of saris, of maidens with water pots on their heads, of dusty plains and snowy mountains and the blazing sun. We had needed no persuading to go!

Islamabad lies one thousand miles north of Karachi. It is bounded by the most spectacular mountains in the world. The Hindu Kush, the Karakoram Range, the Pamirs and the mighty Himalayas. Behind them lay Afghanistan, Russia, China and Nepal. To the east lay India and in the south west was Iran. For Colin it had military, personal, historical and contemporary interest........and within minutes we were about to land there.

Times had changed since those olden days. Pakistan had separated from India at Partition. Uneasy neighbours and suspicious of each other's intentions there had been three wars between them. Pakistan now had a military dictatorship. It became very clear that the military were in evidence as we flew in over Islamabad Airport. As the wheels touched down we could see tents, vehicles and soldiers encamped inside the airport boundary. They had a permanent look about them. Armed with rifles, Airport Police stood by the aircraft steps, sheds and hangars. We were carefully scrutinised as we made our way to the airport terminal and as we emerged by the local population waiting by the barrier.

It was still early morning when we landed on that late September morning. The local citizens were on their way to work. Men dressed identically in loose fitting long cotton shirts and baggy trousers were shuffling along the road. They wore an assortment of scarves and cloths wound around their heads, whilst fixed to their feet and bony ankles were leather sandals that looked several sizes too big. Others sat in groups on their heels by the side of the road with nothing to do but to watch the world pass by. The road was edged by a few sheds and stalls. On the dusty fringes bullocks wandered in amongst some cyclists, whilst donkeys and carts trotted by, their drivers crouched low over the reins. Life starts early in hot countries. It was a world of men. I could see no women walking by the road, driving cars or selling in the roadside stalls. I became increasingly aware of the bold stares from the window of the local bus by the dark skinned inhabitants.

We were instantly struck by the appearance of a new metal beast that hurtled down the road blasting its horn. It was the Pakistani bus. It had every square inch of its tin sides painted in garish colours and it had pieces of material flapping from every corner. It tore down the road with dozens of people hanging on to rail, step and roof in amongst their bundles and bags. The other item of interest was the "Jungly" or lorry, another gaily coloured creation made of what looked like biscuit tins with high sides and narrow proportions that looked unsafe and unsteady in a high wind.

So we arrived in the garden city of Islamabad, with its tree-lined avenues and flowering shrubs. The buildings were modern and clean, an oasis after the dusty drive from Rawalpindi. Here the buses disgorged their passengers who swung their blankets about them and went off to work.

We turned north towards the ridge of hills and down a shady road. There, set among the trees and shrubs in a spacious garden was our house. It was very big by English standards. It was surrounded by a well kept garden full of tropical trees and shrubs. It had balconies and verandahs and clouds of purple bougainvillaea climbing over the walls. As we drew up to the door we could see our staff waiting for us. We had a total of six! Maqbool the cook, Aslam the bearer, and Abdul Rachmann the gardener, who also stood watch by the gate. The other three we were told lived out. They were Razak the driver, Karim the dhobi and Hassan the sweeper. We would meet them later on. It was very daunting! I had never had any staff before and having to manage six men, all of whom knew their jobs much better than I did, was very intimidating. They no doubt felt as apprehensive as I. A new Sahib and Memsahib could make their life as difficult for them as they could for us. They were going to have to show me what I was to expect from them! We hoped that we were going to like each other. As we got out of the car to shake hands I felt relief flood over me. They looked nice. They smiled, genuinely pleased to see us. They lifted our luggage out of the car and up to our rooms, and then vanished discreetly away. No orders were required for the moment. We were sharing the house with our predecessors for a week, so I could watch to see how the house was run.

The house was huge to our eyes. Even more so without the personal effects of the present incumbents who had by this time dispatched their crates. The reception rooms were very big. What sort of parties were we expected to have here? What sort of people would come? How could we ever make it home? There was so much space and so many walls to fill. A gigantic dining room table awaited, its fourteen attendant chairs drawn up to it ready to be laid for some formal dinner party. Suddenly I was very unsure of myself entertaining on this scale. A very large pile of invitations were waiting on the hall table. A feeling of dismay assailed me. We were not professional diplomats. We had been cast in a role that was unfamiliar, in a production of which we knew nothing! No doubt we would soon learn.

At the rear of the house were the staff quarters. Each of the living-in staff had a bare room with stone floors with a string bed or charpoy, a table, a fan and a heater. That was all. Each room was no bigger than a walk-in larder and as bleak and dreary, I was appalled. How could they accept living in such poor conditions? We learned later that most of them lived in mud huts and so to have a room of their own, fans, and heaters in winter were luxuries.

The front garden presented a more encouraging aspect. The verandah led to the lawn. A eucalyptus tree had an attendant crowd of noisy sharp billed crows that were flinging down long pods. In the corner was an oleander tree with beautiful pink sprays intertwined with a vine that climbed along the low wall that edged the drive. A shaggy banana tree with huge flappy tattered leaves cowered shamefacedly against the wall, its brood of bananas the only justification for its existence. There were roses, zinnias, African marigolds and strange velvety crimson flowers that pointed fingers to the sky. We may not as yet have anybody to sit at our table but I would have some lovely flowers to put on it.

As last, reaction set in. Weariness after the long journey, a dismay and disappointment at some of what we had found here, and an apprehension as to how we were going to like and adjust to our new life in this strange land swept over me. The uprooting from home, the parting from our four children and new grandson, none of whom we could expect to see for fifteen months welled up as we unpacked our few possessions. I gazed at their happy smiling faces in their photographs on my dressing table, and I turned to Colin in a blur of tears, deeply thankful for his dear familiar face.

We Get Our Bearings

We had further opportunities the next day to explore our immediate locality and to look at the other houses down our road. We had as neighbours Egyptians, Swiss, Americans, Russians, Pakistanis and Koreans. We all had large flat roofed houses with verandahs, balconies and shady gardens. What intrigued me was the network of aerials, wires, antennae and radio masts that adorned every roof top. Some were hidden behind the houses, others had them bristling for all to see. There would seem to be enormous telegraphic activity going on. I could imagine little men with earphones on, tucked secretly away tapping out messages and codes.

A Russian house across the way from us was guarded by a group of police dressed in navy blue uniforms. Beside them was a very dilapidated tent. Moth-eaten and frayed, it was covered in mud thrown up by the rainstorms. The police on duty stood about holding rifles with bayonets fixed. I saw as the days went by bayonets used for scratching legs, picking finger nails and unstitching a pair of trousers! On one occasion I watched a guard outside an Embassy standing rigidly to attention with his face covered in bubbles and foam while his face was shaved for him! Life was pretty slack for them in our road so that the police spent much time chatting to the chowkidars (watchmen) or making tea.

As we walked down the road all the chowkidars and malis (gardeners) were sitting on the roadside wrapped up in shawls. They had little to do all day but to look for some diversion down the road. My European dress attracted their attention. My bare legs caused the roadside squatters a flutter of excitement. Like naughty schoolboys they whispered behind their hands, the attention of the soldiers across the road was attracted and teeth gleamed among the beards. Indignant and embarrassed at their blatant scrutiny I would make sure I was suitably covered up next time.

Up in the hills behind Islamababd

We drove up the Margalla Hills behind our house where we could see the geometric layout of the city below. The Margalla Hills run from east to west and could be described as the foothills of the western extremities of the Himalayas where they joined the Hindu Kush. To the east we could see the large imposing government buildings, the Diplomatic Enclave where the biggest Embassies were, and the Rawal Lake in the distance. To the west we caught our first glimpse of the Faizal Mosque, still under construction. It was the biggest mosque outside Saudi Arabia. Beside the huge arched roof were the pencil slim minarets, and to one side the new University.

To the south we could see Rawalpindi where in time the two cities would merge when the final building of Islamabad was completed. After Partition in 1947 Karachi was the seat of government but it was decided by the government to move to the north and build a completely new city. It would be closer to the mass of population and to a more comfortable climate. It would also be near to the Great Trunk Road that ran from Lahore to Peshawar.

Building began in 1964 with the Government buildings followed by the larger Embassies with their residences.

Behind us were the pine clad foothills with little isolated villages clustered at their base. Inviting tracks and roads led to mud caked huts perched on the hillside. Smoke rose from their hearths and voices carried up the valley. A brand new city was separated by a few short miles from the lives and homes of village people whose way of life had remained unchanged through the centuries.

Now that we had got our geographic bearings it was time to acquaint ourselves with our new life and with those with whom we were to live. The Service attaches meet each other at regular intervals in each other's homes. A Stag lunch is given on a rotational basis each month when matters of common interest are discussed, like precedence, distribution of moneys, Attache tours, programmes etc. As a group they are invited to Diplomatic functions and Pakistani military functions. This repeated association forms a close brotherhood of companionship and military respect. Saying farewell to these close friends was always sad since the chances of meeting or serving together again were remote. When one of their number leaves station collections made during the year are converted into gifts of a "Box". The farewell party is known as a "Box" party.

The function at which we made our debut was the "Box" party for our predecessor. Held at the home of the Australian Attache, it was attended by Attaches from USA, Ghana, Japan, Turkey, The Soviet Union, France, Germany, Egypt, Indonesia, Malaysia, and Thailand. The Dean of the Corps of Service Attaches from the Soviet Union, appointed by length of service in station not by rank, gave a farewell speech to which a reply was given. The gift was presented, in this case a gun, since Colin's predecessor was a shooting man. A beautiful set of amethyst jewellery was given to his wife... It was a very friendly evening and we were made most welcome. Luckily they all spoke English beautifully, the common language among us all.

As we departed we encountered our first thunderstorm. Ominous banks of cloud had built up over the hills during the afternoon and had settled over the town. There was continuous lightning and thunder. Lashing rain drenched the garden and the trees thrashed wildly about. Rainwater poured off the roofs, flooding the gutters, and formed rivers in the road. The late monsoon was making itself felt.

It was during this first week that we attended our first Reception. It was at the Japanese Ambassador's Residence. Dressed in our finery we swept into the Japanese Embassy Compound, past the guards and police and joined the lines of limousines and staff cars liberally sprinkled with flags and CD plates waiting to drop their guests. Our turn came to alight, and a charming and courteous Japanese servant opened our doors. We mounted the steps and joined the line of guests waiting to shake hands with the Ambassador and his wife in the foyer. We had a chance to look at our surroundings as we waited. The Japanese people furnish their homes with charming simplicity. A beautiful lacquer table here, an ikebana flower arrangement there, and a picture on the wall depicting misty Japanese mountains over there. It was all very restrained and gave a feeling of space. However there was nothing restrained about the charm and courtesy of our Japanese hosts who welcomed us with gracious gestures and friendly words.

As we moved into the large drawing room we realised what an international group we had joined. There were people from all over the world. The women from Japan with their serene faces wore glorious kimonos, the ladies from India with their dark hair parted in the middle and red spot on their foreheads, wore their exquisite saris in mauves and greens and pinks. The large cheerful and jolly ladies from Ghana and Nigeria whose chocolate coloured faces broke out into irresistible smiles, wore their orange, brown and blue robes with matching scarves that swooped up and tied on their heads. The

Reception at Ghanaian Embassy. Colin, Phyllis Ofuso Apea, Sir Oliver Forster (British Ambassador), Self and Larry Ofuso Apea

Pakistani ladies, the first we had had contact with, were wearing their delighful shalwar chemise, most elegant in black with silver thread or emerald silk with gold threading. There were costumes from Malaysia, Thailand, Turkey, Indonesia and a host of others. It was not so easy to identify the nationalities of the western ladies in their evening dress. By contrast the males looked dowdy in their plumage. There were no uniforms on this occasion.

Into this sea of faces we had to make our way, smiling at everybody and nobody in particular. We hoped that somebody would introduce us. A tray of soft drinks was brought up. Coca Cola, orange juice, and 7up! It was obvious that there would be no alcoholic assistance to aid the proceedings. Unidentifiable food on skewers, meat on sticks, puffs and dips were all handed around, each with a paper napkin. Within a short time my handbag was full of napkins, so at a suitable moment I hid them behind a pot plant!

We met new people, we were introduced to others, and recognised by one or two more. Faces came and went, and the moment I met someone else the name of the first people had gone! Some I thought I had remembered but when I met them again I had not a clue who they were! We got some covert stares from the old timers keen to see who the new D.A. was. By the end I was confused and exhausted. It would take months to unravel the jumble of names and nationalities. Why didn't we all wear our names on our chests?

The Japanese Ambassador and his wife were standing where we had left them. I was surprised that the only part that a host and hostess played at their Reception was to say hello and goodbye! At least we knew where to find them. Razak our driver with the staff car was summoned to the front door to collect us by means of a microphone. A highly efficient system of clearing the guests.

It had been a fascinating evening. We had represented our Embassy. We felt rather proud!

The rest of the week was a whirl of people, places and parties. It seemed that all we had to do was to enjoy ourselves. We had no idea where we went, who we met or why. We were swirled about town in the staff car, deposited here and there and then picked up again. I was drowned in the vast quantity of drink consumed, overloaded with mountains of food, and totally defeated by the endless new faces and names. Until I could collect myself and my memory I was wondering how long people would be patient with my blank expression!

Finally the handover week was gone, our predecessors flew away, and we were on our own.

The Monsoon

The clouds drift up
Gathering in heaps over the hills
Ascending ever higher.
Spectacular cloud mountains
Soar up to the heavens.
Then later.......
The storm approaches
A damp grey blanket
Turning day to dusk
Settles over house and town.
A rustle of brittle leaves
Warns beware.
Within the clammy shroud
Thunderous roars and muffled thumps
Reverberate overhead
Until,
Bursting to escape,
The waters of birth
Split the heavens open
And drop their load of rain.
In drenching torrents
And cascading sheets
The rain swirls down,
Lashing winds and thrashing trees
Twigs and branches lie in sodden disarray.
Cars like speedboats tiptoe through the gushing tides.
Then
Its anger spent
The storm moves on,
The waters eddy and hurry away.
The weary leaves lift their heads,
The heavy flower heads shed their tears
And wait soaked and steaming
For the sun.

The Servants Try Us On

The staff presented us with a problem within an hour of being on our own. As we sat in the drawing room trying to draw breath, a soft tap was heard at the door. It was Aslam the bearer holding a telegram.

"What is the matter?" Colin asked.

"Sahib a telegram has come for Maqbool," he told us.

"What does it say Aslam?" we asked.

"His grandmother has died," he replied.

"Have you shown it to Maqbool?" Colin asked him.

"Maqbool no read English," replied Aslam.

"You had better ask him to come in," we told him.

Maqbool came silently into the room wearing his white uniform, his brown feet in flip flops. Maqbool was a very shy man. He preferred to stay in the back ground. He may rule his territory in the kitchen with a vituperative tongue, treating with disdain all those that he considered beneath him but if summoned to the front of the house he became completely docile, the picture of meekness and servility. We explained to him the contents of the telegram. We waited to see his reaction. We could not fathom what he was thinking. Was there a glimmer of a smile on his face? Not exactly the reaction of a man who has lost his grandmother! Was it all a conspiracy? Had it all been planned so as to take advantage of the new unsuspecting Sahib? Very likely! On the other hand, it was possible that his grandmother had died!

Being new to the game there was little else to do but to speed him on his way home. We were perfectly aware that it might have been us who were being taken for the ride!

Our house in Islamabad

Many of the servants who work in Islamabad live several hours' journey away, in Azad Kashmir, Lahore and beyond, and Murree. As Islamabad was created and developed, so jobs became available and bus loads of people came to seek their fortunes in the new capital. Into homes and Embassies they found their way to be trained as drivers, cooks and bearers or to be employed as sweepers, gardeners or watchmen. Because of the distance and the costs involved, they tended to accumulate their days off over a month and then have five days' holiday. Both Maqbool and Aslam lived five hours' journey away beyond Lahore. We sent up heartfelt prayers that Maqbool would return. I was not anxious to have to replace servants so soon.

Whispers must have gone round the staff that the new Sahib was a soft touch, because then it started. One morning on my daily foray into the kitchen to see about food for the day, I found on the kitchen table an array of bed rolls and bedding. My heart missed a beat. Were they all moving out?

"Memsahib we are cold at night."

Maqbool and Aslam like two small boys outside the headmaster's study, stood with their hands behind their backs trying to look as cold and as badly done by as possible. "Our bedding is old. Brigadier Sahib bought for us many years ago."

Colin was invited to look at the offending bed rolls. Certainly they looked threadbare. If that was all they had between them and a charpoy on a frosty night I could see the problem.

It is the responsibility of the employer to see to and make sure that his staff are equipped with uniforms, bedding, fan heaters and in some cases tea and sugar. The limits to which one goes when providing for the staff is a personal matter. It seemed that this one was our responsibility. "Go and get one each and let me see them together with the bill," Colin told them.

They got their bed rolls.

The next episode occurred on wash day when Karim the dhobi came. He had obviously heard that Sahib was dispensing largesse. A brown face with a woolly hat on peered around the kitchen door. In his hand he held an iron. "No good Memsahib, no work."

"What is the matter Karim?" I asked brightly.

"Don't know Memsahib, it's very old."

"All right Karim I have another one you can have," and I dived into the store where I kept a new iron brought out from England. I presented it to him, expecting his face to light up. My beautiful new iron was stared at with distaste.

"Memsahib, no good." he said slowly.

"What's wrong with it?" I asked downcast that my lovely new iron was being discarded out of hand.

"This one good," and he handed me the old one. Weighing about the same as four flat irons of the olden days he obviously considered my light weight one quite useless.

"All right Karim, I'll ask my husband about it."

Karim got his new iron. He may have sold the old one, or kept it for all I knew.

Abdul Rachmann was not to be outdone. Watchman and gardener, he lived outside by the gate for most of the day, and stayed out at night until we returned home. A devout Moslem, he rose at 4am to say his prayers. He watered the garden and picked my flowers for the house long before anybody was about. He lived with Maqbool and Aslam in the servants' quarters behind the house. He had little to do at the front gate so he spent much of his time in a low wicker chair discussing the activities of the house with the neighbouring chowkidars. Having once worked for the Russians across the road we were told he had been planted in our house to report on what went on there. Certainly we had reason to believe that interest in our affairs was being passed on, when I found one day the contents of the waste paper baskets emptied onto the kitchen table and being minutely inspected. Bank statements, letters from home with addresses that could come in useful, though torn up, were being pieced together. Conversations could be over-heard at meal times, and the inyitations in the hall spoke of our social activities. We soon learned to be careful about what we said and where. Also what we left lying about.

Abdul Rachmann wanted new shoes. While a spending spree was on he thought he would try his luck. A battered pair of shoes on an equally battered pair of feet were stuck out for inspection. They spoke for themselves. Abdul Rachmann could not be seen for dust as he tore off down the road to the market to get a new pair. He must have kept them to go home in, he certainly didn't wear them in house or garden.

A little later, delighted with his success, he decided to try again, this time to get some new clothes for gardening....he didn't get them!

Razak, Aslam, Abdul, Rachman, Karim, Hassan and Maqbool

I found all the staff were well trained and they had a routine that worked. It was easier than I had imagined to take on this houseful. It was refreshing to find that they were very discreet and respectful in every way, neither expecting favours nor conversation. They treated us as Sahibs and they expected us to behave as such.

Amongst themselves they had their own order of seniority which was strictly adhered to. There was a definite demarcation line between the cook, bearer, sweeper and the gardener. The dhobi kept to himself in the tiny wash room, coming in only twice a week. Maqbool would never dream of washing up his own pots and pans. He was the No 1 boy, so Aslam the bearer had to do that! Aslam also had to make the beds, lay the tables, wash up, and attend to things from the table upwards. The sweeper crouched down among the buckets and cloths, wiping the marble floors, hoovering or brushing carpets, cleaning baths and loos and sweeping up the leaves on the drive. Abdul Rachman would only sweep them up on the lawn!

Maqbool took his orders from me as he followed me around the house. Hands behind his back, he was a model of servitude while instructions were given. Everything was noted and then passed on to the pair of hands required to do it. No sooner had the kitchen door closed behind him than Maqbool let fly at his troops like a Regimental Sergeant Major gesticulating and barking orders. They vanished in a lather of buckets, dusters and polish! No-one argued with Maqbool. I soon discovered that if he came in in the morning in a sour mood with an unshaven chin, a thunderous black cloud descended on the kitchen and the other staff did well to creep about and keep out of sight.

Often I hoped that he might come up with some suggestions as to what we might eat. Glumly I would stand by the fridge or freezer trying to think up something for him to cook.

"What shall we have today Maqbool?" I would say, hoping that he would have some ideas.

"What you like Memsahib," he would reply.

We were back to square one.

As time went on I enjoyed going into the kitchen to cook myself. Having been trained to cook by the previous Mems who had imparted their own ideas I had to show him that I could cook a bit too! Without being told he would collect up all the utensils I needed, measure all the ingredients and the spoons would be handed to me. He would take it all in with his beady eyes. He could neither read nor write so he had never read a recipe in his life, but I knew that if I asked him to make it himself it would appear on the table exactly as I had shown him. Trained in a Swiss household, he was a natural and an excellent cook.

One day I was mystified when I went into the kitchen. Maqbool was very insistent that I give him some rope. Whatever did he want it for? Was he hanging out some clothes? Tying up his bed roll? The mystery was cleared up when I saw what he was making. He wanted some cotton thread to tie up some beef olives!

I was told the story of a Memsahib in India a few years ago. Apparently it was a large house and the kitchens were some distance from the dining room. The Mem was tired of always having cold food after it had been carried down the long passages. "Why don't you use the hatch?" she suggested to the bearer. At the next dinner party to the astonishment of the assembled guests the hatch opened, a tray was pushed through.......followed by a pair of black legs!

I was fascinated to find in the back of the kitchen drawer an old order book. The Memsahibs of olden times must have left the cook to write out the vegetable order......!

From old shopping lists written by the cook found in Memsahib's kitchen drawer

carats	graeps	tomto
garrets	graps	totmto
	orags	temto
anion	orgets	magos
onyon		maggos
eniuin	garaforat	plumps
eneun	chkakn	plumes
onuin	apal	blubs
oinion	appall	
cabig	tarnaps	peair
kabij	bononas	
kabaj	banaa	potots
cabje	bana	patota
cebaag	bein	
	biness	lama
passely		laman
pasle	suagr	
	spanch	malien
koliflor	sapench	
colefloor	spinack	pippers
		poppers

Shopping in Islamabad

Each of the sectors had its own shopping area and here the planners had worked out a sensible scheme. Modern shops with open plan arcades and accessible parking made shopping easy. Here, as everywhere, life went on in the open. Someone may be crouched over a fire cooking nuts, or mending shoes, selling fruit or doing odd jobs with a bicycle or machine. Your business is their business. There was an unselfconsciousness and a camaraderie among the people on the dusty pavements. Here, there was time for everybody.

There was a preponderance of jewellers and it was an occasion to be savoured when visiting one. Plush seats await, time must be taken and tea; the courtesies were extended and observed before even your interest or intention is known.

A jeweller's shop was a warm or cool comfortable sanctuary in which to sit and observe the rich as they conducted their business.

Jewellery is big business in Pakistan. The dowry of a bride can involve providing up to 200 sets of what to western eyes are rather large and over ornate necklaces, earrings, brooches, bracelets and rings. Many precious and semi precious stones are mined in Pakistan. Emeralds up the Swat valley, topaz in Gilgit, garnets in Chilas, rubies in Hunza and lapis lazuli across the border in Afghanistan. The list of stones was endless and such was the fun of looking for a favoured stone and choosing from a multitude of settings of gold, silver or platinum. I was surprised to find my jewellery valued at UK prices was

valued considerably lower in Islamabad, purely on the accessibility of stones.
We wandered in and out of handicraft shops selling onyx articles from Quetta, leather bags, belts, wallets from sheep and cobra skins, ornate carved wood platters, plates, vases, boxes, spoons and trays. Brass jars, candleholders, ornaments and pots. Bone and ivory birds, elephants, necklaces and earrings, boxes and trinkets and pretty coloured papier maché boxes from Kashmir. Kaftan cottons and wrap around skirts, charming little embossed, engraved or enamelled pill boxes. There was so much to absorb, enjoy and buy and luckily time enough to consider what articles in the long run would be suitable to take up residence in an English cottage.

We had a large hall and landings in the house and walls to fill. The brass and copper shops provided a treasure house of glittering polished bowls, trays, Kashmiri kettles, pots, vases, boxes, hookas and ornaments and Queen Mary Christmas boxes. In 1914 Princess Mary gave to her loyal subjects in India a small rectangular brass box with her effigy on the top containing small comforts. The originals have now become collector's pieces and modern manufacturers are growing fat on fakes.

The Aabpara Market was a happy hunting ground for textiles. Outside the shops, swirls and lengths and bales and bolts of every conceivable type of

The Aabpara Market

27

cottons, prints, silks, lace, suitings and shirtings beckoned us inside. There sitting behind the counter and squatting on the floor were attendant acolytes sipping tea. Several pairs of dark eyes watched as we walked in and leapt to life as we stopped to finger or pull out a bolt.

"What do you want?"

"How much you want?"

"Just looking," we said, looking at chiffons, wools, linens and velveteens.

To cool us down a fan twirled overhead and too late I realised I had on a circular skirt that lifted to the winds and battle began to control my skirt. The Mem's discomfiture was noted and frowned on by shrouded Begums and wide eyed children. The decision to buy was taken. The owner of the shop who up until then had proudly displayed his wares lost interest totally the moment he had made a sale. Summoning his Number 2 with the flick of a thumb he made off to the till. Number 2 measured and cut the required length. With a flourish he then threw the cut length down the counter to Number 3 who picked it up, wrapped it and went it back up the line to Number 1 who when completed the transaction. Maybe if we employed the same tactics in shops in UK the unemployment figures would plummet. As we walked out the scene settled

Siesta!

back to its former drowsy chat and tea drinking.

There was nothing we could not buy in town, and have almost anything made. The Pakistanis are the most obliging and helpful people. They will try to make, construct, repair and fix anything. It is another matter if what they have done breaks, does not work or even falls to bits. They actually want to help and put themselves out for us, an attitude surely to be commended. Though their expertise may sometimes have been suspect, their willingness was a joy.

A thriving and most sought after group in the town were the dherzis or dress makers. In nooks and crannies, in alcoves and attics, the dherzi population sew away, sitting cross legged on the ground pounding away at prehistoric sewing machines. My sewing machine was an antique friend of mine but looked streamlined and modern compared to theirs. Their paint had long since gone with wear and usage but they still ran smoothly with age. Shirts and shalwars were run up within hours. One dherzi we knew could make three shirts in a day. Some like to work on their own premises, others like to work in ours. Cross legged for hours impervious to cramp they sew on. The floor is their table. Without patterns to guide them they can copy anything. The quality and cost of their work is as varied as the workers themselves. Vague suggestions are turned into gorgeous creations and what was a length of material in the shop that morning, by evening could be gracing an Ambassador's table. No wonder we changed our dresses so often. It was a combination of climate, custom and cost. Some dherzis took a pride in finishing their work off, others were content to do little but machine the edges together with the minimum effort.

The older dherzis with a lifetime reputation working for diplomats take a pride and their time to do a beautiful job. Abdul is such a one.

Abdul was the Ambassador's dherzi. He lived and worked, when in Islamabad, at the Ambassador's Residence. A queue of people asked for his services and when your time had come to have him, Abdul requested that his machine be collected and taken to your house. The next morning he arrives on his bicycle carrying a little bundle containing a gigantic pair of scissors, threads, spools. A little corner to work in is all that he asks and he settles himself down cross legged on an old sheet. Then from a rough drawing, a picture from a magazine or a look at an old dress, Abdul can then cut out a perfect pattern with newspapers and in no time is busy snipping and pinning and asking for a fitting. The only time I have ever seen him animated was when he caught sight of my old black Singer. His eyes lit up and he asked me what

I was going to do with it when I go.

"Why, do you want it when I go Abdul?" I asked.

"Yes I want it," he said. "Don't give to anybody else."

I felt honoured that this dear old man should consider my machine a replacement for his.

Behind the tidy facades we found crafts of every kind going on in the open. In cobbled yards entered through an archway another world awaits. Here was a hive of industry. Charpoys were being constructed, a pile of legs propped up against a wall. These are little more than a wooden frame with string woven across. Nowadays a modern charpoy can be seen using a metal frame with wide webbing criss-crossing it. There were pretty bowls, tubs, dishes and water pots stacked up in piles. A framing shop carried on its business; glass, frames and technicoloured pictures leaned against a table and at its feet the dirt and refuse steamed and rotted. The "London Tailor" invited us to enter through a door made of old crates to an attic. Stalls were piled with dates, dried fruits, nuts and ginger. A man sold plastic flip flops, zips and ribbons.

Shoe making for the private customer is an art that has almost ceased to exist in England due to prohibitive costs. In Pakistan plentiful supplies of leather enable boot and shoe makers to carry on their craft and fashion shoes for every member of the family.

In a little alcove square-toed chapplies hung on the door and wall told us we had found our goal. There sitting cross legged on the floor surrounded by shoe moulds, glue, threads and scraps of leather sat Mohammed. Mohammed had been making shoes for years. He sat in the doorway of his shop, no bigger than a cupboard, with a woolly cap on his head. His cheerful, friendly face was surrounded by grey whiskers. When he saw us he beamed at us.

"Come in. Sit down," he waved us inside.

A broken plastic bench already crowded was cleared for us.

"What you want? I will make for you."

We gazed around at the dozens of pairs of sandals poking out of dusty shelves and hanging from strings. The thick, clumpy all purpose everlasting chapplies. Not quite what I was wanting.

"Can you copy these?" I asked him, showing him my old battered court shoes.

"What colour you want?" He clicked his fingers to some invisible apprentice.

We watched two men working and marvelled at how shoes came to be made at all and how they looked so professional after they had been carved out of leather, sewn, hammered, glued and stitched up with the most basic of tools.

Feet and toes were used to hold cutters or glue brushes. The samples were brought back.

"These do? " he asked.

Our choice was made. My foot was used as a template on his order book and a measurement was taken.

"Come back one week," he said. One week later I was the proud possessor of a smart pair of shoes. Cost? £6!

Mahommed the shoe maker

The opportunity to have personal services done without dismaying delays or costs, by a plentiful supply of people whose pleasure it was to oblige was indeed a great joy. The town abounded with workmen and craftsmen who were available and accessible. The watchmaker in his shop was able and willing to repair and return within days.

The cabinet maker and the carpenter had their workshops on the premises. We watched them at work. Everywhere people were busy and working for themselves in countless tiny businesses. Later traders would come to the door selling carpets, pictures, brass and copper. Roadside vendors, their little carts piled high with fruits, oranges, apples and bananas were free to ply their trade. Small children ran up to us in the car park with a fistful of combs and hairpins in their grubby hands. Beseeching faces peered through the car window, fingers pointing to their mouths; the unmistakeable gesture for baksheesh. Everyone tried to make money where they could.

Sometimes the will to work exceeded the ability to carry it out. We took some silver to Rawalpindi to have it replated, also one of our candelabra had been bent in transit from UK and the centre piece wobbled about, unstable and unsafe for use at dinner parties. "No problem," was the answer.

"You must make it firm and strong," we insisted.

"OK OK!" was the answer.

Later that week we returned. All the silver plate looked lovely! The candlestick stood firm and strong. We were delighted but only until we got it home and wanted to fit a candle inside it. It worked loose and we saw it had been fixed together with a rusty nail inside for support and then glued together. Once loosened, and with every movement there trickled out a few more lumps of white powder that for all the world resembled polyfilla. Our candlestick resumed its drunken stance propped up at the back of the cupboard.

Another occasion was the installation of the telephone. We wanted to put an extension up in our bedroom which entailed threading a lead up from the telephone in the hall. The workmen arrived and I explained where the extension was to be installed. "Ji" they said. I left them to it. A little later I was invited to check. Had they finished already? It seemed very quick. Proudly they showed me what they had done. Instead of fixing the wire neatly up each step and securing it along the skirting of the walls I found it had been laid loose up the stairs, diagonally across the landing on top of the rugs and on into our bedroom. They had brought fifty yards too much wire. The idea of cutting it did not occur to them. The remaining wire had been trailed back across the bedroom floor and finding nowhere to put it, they had laid it across the landing again. They then proceeded to wind, thread and weave the remainder of the black wire in and out of the white wrought iron bannisters.

Friends of ours had to have a new shower put in over the bath. The shower people were called in to fix it up. To their astonishment they found fixed to the ceiling not one, but two shower heads, one at each end of the bath! One was for hot water, the other for cold!

Murree

Thirty miles east of Islamabad is the hill station of Murree. It is 7000 ft above sea level. It was to Murree and Simla and the other hill stations that the heat-weary residents from all over India migrated to escape the blazing heat in summer. The lure of the Himalayas with their majestic snowy peaks, the snowscapes of Kashmir with the scent of the pine forests proved irresistible to those from cooler climes. Those who spent long years of service in the subcontinent endured the baking heat of the plains year after year. They came to cool down, relax and rest their eyes on unbelievable views, pineclad mountains, flowering shrubs and damp dewy grass.

The British annexed the Punjab in 1849 and it was because of the importance of the military cantonments in and around Rawalpindi that Murree was developed in 1851. In local dialect 'Marhi' means a high place. It had an ideal location with spectacular views to the north, south, east and west.

A little England grew up. Bungalows sprouted up on the hill tops and ledges, their windows and balconies angled to the best view and light. For six months of the year Murree came to life. Luggage boxes and all the paraphernalia needed for a long sojourn in the hills had been pushed, heaved or carried to the top. Those that returned every year made sure that they built their homes on all the best sites.

Soldiers stationed at Rawalpindi in the 1880's marched to Murree in three days. Lucky ones went by tonga (horse drawn cart) that took six hours!

Those that came from further afield had to come to the rail head at Rawalpindi and carry on by horse cart or on foot.

Wives of the officers of the military or government departments continued the life they had led in the plains. There were lunches, dinners, tea parties and bridge. With husbands away, lonely wives amused themselves with illicit affairs. There was riding, golf and sports of all kinds. Ayas looked after the children who roamed and scampered among the forest trails and in the cool streams.

In 1860 Lawrence College was founded for the orphans of the British soldiers killed in the Indian Mutiny. Founded on British public school lines it is run to this day by Christian missionaries and teachers. Familiar amenities had to be preserved. A church was established and a Mall for promenading. Hotels called the Metropole, Viewforth and The George were built. Cafes, parks, shops, clubs and sporting facilities were set up for the amusement of the British who tended to keep themselves to themselves. Servants could be obtained for the sum of Rs 5.00 (25 pence) a month from the surrounding areas. There was natural water in the hills, but despite all efforts to prevent it cholera broke out every three or four years. Because of this the then Lieutenant Governor had to shift his HQ to Simla in 1876.

During the widespread turmoil and riots that followed the Partition of India in 1947 hundreds of bungalows were burnt down and several luxurious hotels including the Metropole, Viewforth and The George with their ballrooms and bars were burnt down too.

We travelled to Murree hoping to retrace the steps that Colin's parents would have taken 50 years ago.

The road from Islamabad remained flat and level for about ten miles. Then the road turns north east, and as we began to climb the view unfolded below. Up and up we climbed around hair pin bends, occasionally getting stuck behind buses that carried not only fare paying passengers but several dozen that had sprinted up the road and had leapt on the back! Puffing diesel fumes they ground their way up the hills to petrol stations where both bus and driver were refuelled.

The view was incredible. The lower hills rolled and folded into each other as far as the eye could see to the north and west. We were soon up among the pine trees. Beside the road young trees had been planted to replace timber loss through felling, rockslips or storms.

Around Tret and Ghora Gali hundreds and hundreds of dwellings sprinkled the hillsides and far down into the valley where neither sun nor road penetrated. Some of the old wooden houses, now little more than heaped up piles of firewood, stood with broken casements, cockeyed doors and broken balconies. Washing was draped over the balconies and we wondered how anybody could live in that crumbling edifice. It looked as if one mighty shove, storm or rockslip would send it like a heap of matches to the bottom of the valley. Years ago it must have been a favoured residence. Sadly now all that there was to commend it... was its view.

At the top of the hill we understood why they had come to Murree. Spectacular views towards Kashmir in the north and to the plains in the south stretched as far as the eye could see. A vast community roosted on the ridges and in the valleys that nestled up to Murree amongst the pine trees. Many of the old buildings had been left to run down or rust and now lay abandoned beside the more modern and modest.

That times had changed became apparent as we looked about and saw communication masts, TV booster stations, tourist bureau, municipal buildings, banks and hospitals. There were now eight schools and colleges, eighteen hotels and four rest houses and cinemas! A huge population lived up there!

We tried to imagine the olden days as we wandered down the Mall, now called Jinnah Road. It was a thoroughfare rather different from its counterpart in England. Three hundred yards long, it was no wider than a lane. Two cars could pass with difficulty. All down one side shops sold fur hats and purses, furry waistcoats, shawls from Kashmir, Numdah rugs and tea cosies. There were carved wooden boxes, carpets, brass and mirror work from Sind. We spoke to one old man in one of the carpet shops who remembered the British days and the names of favoured customers! He even remembered the items that they bought! He said that the British were always very fair and kind!

Halfway down the Mall through a wicket gate was the church. In the prime position it could have been transplanted straight from England, with its red brick Gothic arches, bell tower and cross. Inside it was cool, high ceilinged and whitewashed. Brass plaques were fixed to the wall and beautifully polished memorials told of the families who had lost kith and kin. On the walls there was mention of the death of so many young children. One tugged at the heart:- "I wonder where the little faces go that come and smile and stay awhile and then pass like flakes of snow. There is no need to wonder in that bright land so far we shall find those little faces with their guardian angels there". It was in the memory of a little child of two years old.

Looking through the register in the year 1947 so many infants lost their lives aged between nought and four years old. They died of fever, pneumonia, crib death or typhoid. They had possibly been brought up to the healthier climate of the Murree to recover from their sickness. During the years 1922 and 1923 the Staff Sergeants and Lieutenants and Captains produced between them 49 and 48 babies. By 1947 the annual production rate had dropped to six. The first marriage in the church was in 1855 and the last in 1979.

It was not hard to imagine the gathering of bonnets and bustles outside in the church yard, and the ladies in their boaters nodding to friends. Outside the parasols would flutter and twirl as they walked through the churchyard to Lintott's or Sam's restaurants, still there today! A place to rendezvous and to acquaint others of the fact that they had been to church!

By Lintott's the Mall widened out to include a little garden with places to rest in the shade. Had Colin's parents sat there and watched the fountains and listened to the band? We could easily imagine the bandsmen from one of the Regiments entertaining the promenaders as they strolled up and down.

Below the Mall on a lower level was the bazaar. On either side of the steep narrow cobbled pathway the little shacks and sheds, shops and stalls displayed their wares. There were pots and pans, materials, seaweed colour and textured plastic sandals, sweetmeats and soaps. In an alcove bedrolls and quilts were being stuffed.

Sitting on the steps and in the door ways, cross-legged and hunched amid the whirling sewing machines, the dressmakers and tailors ran up shirts and shalwars. Children with dusty hair and grubby clothes played hide and seek among the cabbage stalks and refuse on the path. Out of the sun chilly draughts whistled around the fretwork of the ancient buildings, narrow passages and tumbled down tenements. Glimpses of the distant hills could be seen through archways, alleyways and lanes threaded like mouseholes through this derelict maze. Rags of clothing hanging up over some weatherboard proved the fact that people actually lived in the rickety attics under the rusty corrugated iron roofs and eaves.

Large flat steaming pans filled with purple, pink, green and blue dyes were being stirred by wooden tongs. Chiffon scarves and cotton lengths matched for colour were stretched and shaken and then pinned out across the pathway to dry, blowing like flags in the breeze.

On the other side of the Mall an underground market sold basket work, bales of cloth, trinkets and what looked enough grain, peanuts, walnuts, dates and dried fruit to feed thousands. Mountains of sultanas, currants, chillies, and dried apricots were piled up in sacks and bales from floor to ceiling. Their owners were perched on the sacks shivering in the semi darkness wrapped up tightly in their blankets.

An icy wind whistled relentlessly up the dark passage so we were glad to climb the steps back up to the warm sunshine.

The Telephone Call

ME	Hullo.
HIM	Hullo.
ME	Oh Hullo, is that Mrs Khan's residence?
HIM	Hullo.
ME	Could I speak to Mrs Khan please?
HIM	Hullo Hullo.
ME	Is Mrs Khan there please?
HIM	Mrs Khan?
ME	Yes please.
HIM	Ek minute.
ME	Thank you

INTERVAL OF TWO MINUTES

HIM	Hullo.
ME	Is Mrs Khan there please?
HIM	Huh?
ME	Could you get Mrs Khan please?
HIM	Who do you want?
ME	I want Mrs Khan...
HIM	Hullo
ME	**I want to Speak to Mrs Khan...Please.**
HIM	Who is speaking? What is your good name please?
ME	It is Mrs Watts from the British Embassy.
HIM	This is not the British Embassy.
ME	I am from the British Embassy, I want Mrs Khan...
HIM	You want Mrs Khan?
ME	Yes please..
HIM	Wrong number...

Social Occasions

We were invited to many large receptions, Armed Forces Days and National Days. They were elegant and gracious affairs. Many of them required the Service Attaches to wear their uniforms. It was a splendid sight to see all our men folk in their evening dress regalia. Wearing their Army, Navy and Air Force plumage, their many coloured caps, badges, medal ribbons and gold braid, our husbands from a score of countries looked a very fine sight indeed.

The residences and Embassies to which we were summoned were lit by strands of coloured lights that hung like necklaces over the wall and balconies, and they were threaded through trees and bushes. If it was held in the garden, screens or shamianas were put up for privacy and carpets were laid on the grass.

At the gate all the local chowkidars watched the comings and goings of the guests, familiar by their drivers and staff cars. We would walk up the path on a red carpet edged with candles and lights to the reception line, often brightly lit for photographic purposes. If the President was attending we would have been made aware of it some distance away by the dozens of police lining the route every few yards, and the military police gathered at the entrance.

After shaking hands with our hosts, we would make our way into the teeming throngs of people. Relieved to see those we knew, we were surrounded by those we did not. Since few introductions were made and name tags were not worn, we had to pick up names as best we could and which Embassy they were from. Business folk used these receptions for business purposes and they would bring out their visiting cards with practised hand. Other people would introduce themselves and you hoped to catch their names. Americans are very good at it. They concentrate, they remember the name and then use it. I do concentrate, I do try to remember, but I have immediately forgotten it. I found it very hard to remember Japanese names like Sumiko, Tomiko, and Yoshiko, especially as their owners all looked the same! I was soon having to resort to subterfuge to cover the fact that I could no longer remember the names of people who were kind enough to remember mine.

On parade at a reception

It is at these parties that we would meet them again. Where had we met before? Which Reception? I would chat on hoping for a clue.. Blank! The mental computer registers nothing!... I am treated like an old friend... What on earth IS HER NAME? If she moves on to the next group still under the impression that I did know who she was, I have got away with it.... for the moment. But urgent action had to be taken to rectify the situation.

If I was successful, I would hide behind a pot plant and put their name in my address book... Sometimes I would ask them to write it themselves. "So

---

that I make sure that I can spell it correctly". I was rather proud of this method! When they were not looking I would insert aide memoires like "Frizzy Hair" or "Big grin" or "Eats curry puffs" Then I think I have got it. I am stuck next time if she happens to be eating something else!

A very beautiful Indian lady came up to me at a function. I had met her several times. She knew my name. She certainly didn't have frizzy hair, and she wasn't eating curry puffs. What was I to do? The ideal solution was for somebody else to appear and say "Hallo so and so" to the unidentified one. That would be wonderful. From then on I could use her name all the time. I could even introduce her to somebody else.... but this time she didn't wander away... she stayed where she was. Nobody came up with her name... The worst happened. A friend of mine came up to chat and join in the conversation. It was obvious that they had not met each other. Now I was for it... I had to introduce them. Minutes went by and I put it off. I couldn't admit I didn't know her name!

Then the Indian lady said, "I don't think we have met before, we haven't been introduced."

My cue...This was it... I managed the one name I knew, and then my courage vanished and me with it... With an exaggerated look around the room I said "Please forgive me, there is a lady over there who I want to catch before she leaves, I'll be back in a minute". And vanished! I asked several other people but nobody else knew her name until somebody suggested that we look in the visitors book in the hall.

"I might recognise it," she said. She did.

Hugely relieved I wrote her name in my mind, memory and book. "I am so sorry," I said to the two ladies when I returned, "I dashed off before I could introduce you," and produced the name triumphantly.

Not only did we have to contend with names but countries as well. We were invited to have dinner with a very delightful elderly couple. He was a retired Pakistani General. There were one or two Ambassadors and ministers... and us. I sat next to a small dark man who seemed familiar. We had met him a few days before. We chatted happily over dinner. He was very easy to talk to and he was very friendly and fun. We were having a nice time when I mentioned something about, "Your country Portugal" ... Something had gone badly wrong. There was a chill in the air. I had done it this time. His interest vanished. Pointedly he turned away and started to talk to his neighbour. I was ignored for the rest of the meal. The truth dawned, he was the Indian Ambassador.

Alexandra Fedorov, wife of the Russian senior Attache was leaving after five years. A letter arrived from her inviting me to attend a tea party at her house to say farewell. The ruling regarding our attitude towards the Russians was laid down by the British Embassy. Since the invasion of Afghanistan our relations with the Russians were "cool". We should have no social contact beyond the minimum courtesies at Receptions and parties. We did not invite them to our parties and we did not accept their invitations unless it was a Service Attache function such as the fortnightly wives gathering, a Stag lunch held every month, a Box party or a farewell. Alexandra's invitation I assumed had been extended to all the Attache wives as it was her farewell party.

As I arrived at her house I was surprised to see no other cars parked outside. There were no signs of any other guests beyond one other Russian car with its 62 number plate. Effusively greeted by Alexandra and other Russian wives Ludmilla and Svetlana, I went into the room. There sitting around the edge of the room were indeed one or two Attache wives, Chavanee from Thailand, Isil from Turkey, the predictable Indian wives, the poor sad and silent Afghan wife, and sitting around in glum and stony silence...were fifteen Russian wives including the Ambassador's wife. I was the only Western European there!

Seated in a place of honour I was handed food and drink and a fuss was made. Alexandra's husband came beaming up with a camera and took a close up flash photograph, To be filed away in the Kremlin? Hobnobbing with the Russians? I began to feel that I had let myself into a compromising position. Where were the Americans? The Australians? and the French? Thank goodness the West German wife appeared. She was always very effusive with the Russians and hugged and kissed them at parties. Who else had been invited, but had been told not to attend? Feeling very uncomfortable and wishing that I had cleared it with the Embassy myself beforehand I resolved to get myself out of there as soon as possible.

As soon as tea was announced I made an excuse, and slipped away, but not before I had taken a picture of all of them! Telling Colin about it later he said in the circumstances I was unwise to have gone. From those to whom I spoke afterwards I gathered that they had not been invited... So why me?

Even those to whom we can extend friendship can blow hot or cold depending on the current Diplomatic climate. The Indian Defence Attache was leaving. They had been very charming and friendly over the months and they had even invited us to their daughter's wedding in Delhi. I wanted to say goodbye and give them a little gift. When I went to their house I found the three

Attaches and their wives deep in conversation in the sitting room among the packing cases. Far from the friendly welcome I had had on previous occasions the cold stares I received when I walked in left me in no doubt that my presence was unwelcome. What was the matter? Mystified I assumed that I had interrupted a last minute conference. Mumbling a brief goodbye I handed over the little gift and disappeared.

Ten minutes later I collected a British Embassy wife to take her around town. "Have you heard?" she asked eagerly.

"Heard what?" I replied.

"Because of the Indian Minister who was murdered in Britain, the Indians think that we are indirectly responsible. They have threatened to blow up the British Embassy!"

Defence Attache

As the weeks went by Colin was finding his way about the Defence Section in the Embassy. He was driven to work each day in the staff car by Razak, the very long established driver in the Embassy and who is permanently assigned to the Defence Attache. There is no place or person in Islamabad or Rawalpindi that is unknown to Razak. He can predict the intentions of the DA and what is required of him. Whether waiting for us outside a Reception or in the back streets of Rawalpindi he was a very reassuring sight. He was wholly dependable and reliable and Colin counted himself very lucky to have him.

Life with the DA is not without its hazards. About three weeks before we arrived in Pakistan, Razak was kidnapped up the Khyber Pass. He was driving a party of senior officers from the Royal College of Defence Studies on a visit from London. Part of their tour in Pakistan included a trip through the Khyber Pass up to the Afghan border at Torkham. The then Defence Attache sent Razak on ahead alone in the staff car up the Pass to await the RCDS party who were following on in a bus. They were all to rendezvous at the Officers' Mess of the Khyber Rifles' Mess at Landi Kotal.

A railway winds its way through the mountains and valleys of the pass and it was at a level crossing that Razak had to stop. It was there that two men with carbines pounced on him. He was dragged out of the driver's seat, bundled blindfolded and chained into the back of the car. The bandits then drove both Razak and the staff car away. Where they went Razak had no idea.

They bumped and jolted for miles. The road deteriorated and finally petered out altogether. He was taken to a cave and then hidden in two different huts. For five days he was completely lost.

Meanwhile representations were made by the Government of the North West Frontier Province. The elders of the tribes were called and told to release Razak and the car. If they refused they would be required to pay a hefty fine. This threat must have been sufficient, because at an appointed time a policeman found Razak and the car safe and well but badly shaken.

Why had he been kidnapped? Much illicit heroin was being distilled up in the tribal areas, and the North West Frontier Province governing body were trying to track down the manufacturers and dealers. They were drawing the net nearer. The Pathans, Afridis and others were not known for their tolerance of interference in their affairs. They would often take matters into their own hands and demonstrate independence and muscle. Razak happened to be in the wrong place at the wrong time and he became their unfortunate victim.

The British Embassy stood with the other large Embassies at the Eastern end of the town. Security has been tightened ever since the American Embassy was set on fire in 1979. Anti American hysteria was whipped up at the time of the siege in Mecca. Rumour had it that the Americans had had a hand in that tragic affair. Fanned into a frenzy by the mullahs, a mob of students from Islamabad University bent on revenge stormed the American Embassy during working hours. Surprise was complete. They swarmed over the walls of the compound and set fire to the buildings. Those inside were trapped and as the heat mounted they climbed to the top of the building where they were trapped for many hours. The floors bubbled and the concrete melted. The British Ambassador protested to the President and gave him "Holy Hell" as one American put it. Finally the police and the Army gained control of the mob and those trapped on the roof were released by ladders. Unfortunately, during the fracas, one of the US Marine security guards was killed. The episode left a sense of anger, dismay and concern, not only for the plight of the Americans but for the whole of the Diplomatic community in Islamabad. The Pakistani Government, answerable for the safety of all the foreign missions on their soil, were held responsible for their negligence and for paying the bill for building a new Embassy.

The whole incident left a chastened and subdued American Colony. In the British Embassy the already stringent security measures were tightened even further. Since then there have been no further incidents. But nobody was complacent.

Colin was in charge of the Defence Section. When he was finally in the chair he realised what a bewildering variety of subjects he was going to have to deal with. Not the least with trying to keep abreast of the vast amount of paper work that flowed in. He had to read the Pakistani newspapers and the signals that came in from UK every day. He had to note the visitors coming from England with commercial or military interest. He had to learn about the aid programmes, immigration matters and press reports on such subjects as Afghanistan, World Health and conferences concerning Pakistan. He had to read guidance telegrams from the FCO on many diverse subjects like the Falklands, UN Council meetings, disarmament talks, and US Congress decisions on their military budget. He had to acquaint himself on matters military in Pakistan. He had to arrange military training and academic courses for Pakistani Service students in both military and academic institutions in UK, and plan military visits for those coming from UK. Annually the Royal College of Defence Studies came on tour to Pakistan. Serving and retired Generals come for long or short periods expecting an interesting itinerary to be planned for them.

Ex British Army pensioners caused him much distress. Their meagre pensions no longer sufficient, they pleaded poverty and reduced circumstances. These faithful old soldiers with their unswerving loyalty to the Queen write to their sovereign to whose father they gave their devoted service and allegiance. They now expect her to intervene and provide for their old age, or a one way ticket to UK. There is a Remembrance Day ceremony each year at the War Graves cemetery in Rawalpindi to which all the Commonwealth countries send representatives. Colin had to arrange this.

There were many occasions to take him out of the Office. There were Naval and Air Force parades, and Officer Passing out Parades, not only in Rawalpindi, but also in Abbotabad, Peshawar and Karachi. There were visits to the British Army students in Quetta. A full programme of receptions added to the countless big and small private parties in and around Islamabad. It all seemed quite enough to be going on with.

One of his first assignments out of town was to attend the President's Passing out Parade at Kakul. This was the equivalent of the Passing out Parade at the Royal Military Academy at Sandhurst.

The Academy was 78 miles away at Kakul in Abbotabad, a pleasant town 4000ft up in a fertile valley. It has always been the home of the military. It was built by the British and the cantonment area has its European style bungalows, club, church and cemetery. The Plains to the south and the valley and hills around make an ideal location for training purposes. It now comprises the Headquarters of the Punjab Frontier Force (The Piffers), the Baluch Regiment, the Headquarters of the Army Medical Services, and the home of the Military Bands and Music.

Military Parades are held early in the day in hot countries, and so with some distance to go before the Parade at 9am, we sped westwards up the Grand Trunk Road towards Peshawar. We joined a procession of Staff cars displaying their CD plates with varying numbers of stars depending on the rank of the occupant. A steady stream of brass hats and red tabs and their equivalent in the Navy and Air Force swept along at ease and leisure.

We turned off the Grand Trunk Road at Hasan Abdal for Abbotabad, and were flanked by hills in the distance and Afghan Refugee camps that sprawled over a wide area. The hills narrowed as we drove up the valley, and as we climbed we could see the first signs of habitation round the town of Abbotabad. Parks, gardens and trees lined the roadside as we came into the town. Sign posts pointed to the many military establishments in the town. The Military Police and soldiers were kept busy as all the staff cars motored through. Smart

Colin with Col "Curly" Templeton, Australian Defence Attache,
Pakistan National Day Parade

in their immaculate uniforms, spotless white spats, belts and gloves, they guided us through the town to the Academy.

Colin struggled into his belts and straps as we approached the Parade ground. He adjusted his hat on his head and we waited in the queue to be deposited at the assigned spot. As we alighted a group of Pakistani Officers advanced towards us with a programme and a smart salute. We went up the steps past the guards and the gates to the reviewing stand. We were shown to our very comfortable arm chairs in the front row. Seated beside Colin was the Chinese Attache. It must have been his first parade of that type since he asked Colin when he should sit, stand and salute! He kept a wary eye on Colin all through the proceedings! In front of us was the Parade ground with the Academy laid out on the hill behind it. Hundreds of families were watching from roped off stands.

As we waited for the Parade to begin, there was a flutter of activity as the cameraman who had been showing interest in us all ran off after more exciting quarry. We all stood up as a diminutive figure strode to his position escorted by his staff officers. General Zia ul Haq had arrived to take the Parade. It was our first sight of the President of Pakistan.

It must be an occasion that he enjoyed and one that would take him back to his years as a cadet. He was commissioned into the Indian Army in 1943. He served with the 13th Lancers and with the Guides Cavalry in the North West Frontier Corps. He had led the third military coup in Pakistan's history and had set himself up as President in 1977. Over the years he has become a forceful politician with a tight grip on affairs at home, and his forays into the international scene had been well received. Those that had met him had been impressed with his statesmanship, and regarded him as a benign rather than a malignant dictator. However, having achieved his position by force there are those who are less than enthusiastic about him.

His goal was to have a government based on Islamic principles which would have more universal appeal. With all this in mind we were intrigued to see him in the flesh, mindful too that this was the man who had executed Zulfikar Ali Bhutto. Holding the offices of the Chief of the Army, Marshal law Administrator and the President of Pakistan, he was the most powerful man in the land.

Except for the fact that the faces of the cadets were darker than their British counterparts, the march on, inspection, presentation of the Sword of Honour to the best cadet, the march off of the white horse up the steps to *Auld Lang Syne*, the ceremonial was identical to a Sandhurst Passing out Parade! Even the band played just recognisable English tunes.

When it was all over, the crowd dispersed to various reception areas for refreshments. We walked up the road to the Mess with some of the Cadets relaxed after the Parade that they had practised for months. Their eager faces crowded round Colin, pleased to be spoken to by one of the visiting military. Deferential and keen they looked tough and disciplined. At Kakul they train for four years and are awarded a degree at the end.

We followed the Cadets to their Mess where a vast concourse of people had gathered together. It was an occasion for reunion and reminiscence, also a renewal of acquaintances for the military fathers who had successfully launched their sons.

As the party progressed, the President, surrounded by security guards, mingled with the guests moving from group to group. With my back turned I was unaware how close he had come until suddenly I realised that he was there. With his hand outstretched towards me and his dark rimmed eyes staring was the President of Pakistan.... Taken completely by surprise, I managed to mumble something as I shook his hand. He smiled and was very affable. I told him that our two sons had recently passed out from Sandhurst, one into the Royal Tank Regiment, an affiliated Regiment to his old Regiment 13th Lancers, and the other into the Army Air Corps. He was very interested. He turned to Colin and told him to let him know when Andrew came out to Pakistan as he would like to meet him. It had been an honour to meet the President but I had not welcomed the ogling attention of the crowds who jostled around him. The shy Begums had retreated like a tide as he moved about, and stood like sheep in a pen watching from a safe distance.

Then it was all over. The crowd of security guards, military police and soldiers surged around as he left and the procession of motor bikes and limousines sped off down the hill and away.

It spoke much for the calibre of those old soldiers from Britain who brought with them the best traditions of military turn-out, precision and bearing, that the Services in Pakistan today see fit to perpetuate the customs and ceremonial long after the British have left.

We had been very impressed. There could be no doubt that the British soldiers of old would have been very proud of what we had seen at Kakul.

Pakistani Hospitality

Andrew, our elder son, a Lieutenant in the Royal Tank Regiment based in Germany, planned to bring some soldiers to Pakistan to trek in the Northern Areas. He had been to Pakistan before so he knew where he wanted to go and how to get there. Permission had been granted for the visit by the Ministry of Defence in London, the Foreign Office in Islamabad and the Pakistan Government. The route had been decided and maps and funds made available. Their flight was to bring them as far as Karachi but from there they would have to make their own way north, a thousand miles away. They could use public transport, but timetables were uncertain and the soldiers' schedule tight. The British Embassy Section had only one Land Rover which could be made available to them. Recalling the interest that the President had shown in Andrew's impending visit, Colin decided to ask if another vehicle could be provided by the 13th Lancers in Lahore. A month before Andrew was due to arrive he wrote to the President setting out his request. The weeks went by and there was no word or acknowledgement to his letter.

The day came when Andrew and his men were due to arrive. Failing everything else Razak, Colin's driver had been detailed to go down to Karachi to collect the party and somehow squeeze them into the Land Rover. At midday the phone rang. It was the President's office. They would like Colin to know that Lieutenant Watts and his men would be the guests of the Pakistan Government for the duration of their stay in Pakistan. They would meet them in Karachi.

Later that day, hot and weary and completely unaware of what was waiting for them, Andrew and his soldiers arrived at Karachi Airport. To Andrew's surprise they were told to leave the aircraft by the first class exit. There at the airport steps waiting to welcome them were a Colonel, Lieutenant-Colonel, a Major and a Captain! To their astonishment they were taken to the VIP lounge and from there to stay overnight at the Mid Way Hotel.

Next day they were transported to the airport and flown by Pakistan International Airways to Lahore where they were most royally looked after by the officers and men of the 13th Lancers. They were overwhelmed with kindness and gifts. They were all given Puma track shoes, crested cuff links, silver platters, beautiful illustrated books on Pakistan signed by the President, and Andrew was personally presented with a carpet!

They were brought to Rawalpindi in an air-conditioned coach and put up in the Shalimar Hotel, and from there transported to the British Club where they could relax.

Later they were flown to Gilgit by PIA and from there they were driven across the tracks and trails over which they had planned to trek! Up in the northern areas they were guests of the Chitral Scouts who laid on a display of National Dancing on the quad, which they were invited to join in. Their brief sojourn up in the fort in the mountains remained as one of their most magical of memories.

They hadn't finished yet! Hurried ever onwards they went to Nowshera, the home of the Armoured Corps and at Peshawar were put up at the Khyber Intercontinental Hotel. The final gesture of good will and kindness was to drive them right up the Khyber Pass to the Mess of the Khyber Rifles at Landi Kotal. Here again they were made most welcome. The restrictions had been such that nobody, not even the prestigious Royal College of Defence Studies team had been allowed up the Khyber Pass.

As a final gesture President Zia invited Colin, Andrew and his senior Sergeant to have a private audience with him. For forty minutes they chatted amicably. Andrew suggested that a Pakistan Army hockey team should visit B.A.O.R. coinciding with the Presentation of the Colours to his Regiment there the following year.

The President was most enthusiastic and he promised that it should happen, "While I am in a position to see it done," he added rather ruefully.

Completely overwhelmed in every way by the hospitality of all those they had met, and all that had been done for them, eight weary soldiers boarded the flight to Germany.... wondering how they were going to explain to those

who had sponsored them why they had done hardly any trekking at all....
And all that Colin had asked for was a Land Rover!

We were getting used to the unexpected in Pakistan. We were also
getting used to social occasions happening, or not happening at the last minute.

"Darling, I'm not sure yet but we may have to have dinner with the
President tomorrow," Colin phoned from the Embassy, "The Ambassador is
going and some others from the Embassy. I'll know in the morning if it is to
be us."

There had been a flurry of intense activity in the Embassy with the
imminent arrival of Princess Anne who was on an unofficial visit to Pakistan
to see the Save the Children Fund team at Peshawar. Our commitment was to
go to the Airport to receive her and to attend a reception at the Embassy for her
that evening. The Princess was to go on to have dinner with the President
afterwards.

The next morning, Colin in full military regalia and I went down to
Islamabad Airport to meet the Princess. We waited in a long line on the red
carpet set out on the tarmac. The senior Pakistani dignitaries came first, then
the British Ambassador and his Counsellors. 'To wear a hat or not to wear
a hat' had been the question. When the Princess arrived looking cool and
charming and wearing a hat, I regretted not bringing out my ceremonial
feathers.

Colin snapped up a salute as she passed by shaking our hands. She
walked along lines of children wearing national costume who threw flower
petals in her path; a very delightful custom. She then left in a motor cavalcade
to attend to her other duties before the reception in the evening.

During that morning Colin phoned again. "It's us," he said, "We have
to go to have dinner with the President tonight."

"Anyone else going?" I asked.

"No just the Ambassador and us from the Embassy," he said.

"Why us?" I asked, mystified.

"Must be the military flavour," he replied, and rang off.

What a flurry and a worry! What would I wear? It is not often that we
are invited to dinner with a Princess and a President! It was also not an
invitation that one could refuse. An evening dress was under construction at
a dressmaker. Could he finish it? I raced down to Mahommed sitting cross-
legged in his alcove. "Mahommed could you finish my dress by tonight?!" I
panted.

"OK Memsahib, I bring it to you."

There were other readjustments to be made for the evening. The afternoon flew by. I washed my hair. The dress arrived rolled up in a grubby cloth. I had to wash it. An hour later with the dress still damp in places we were ready to go to the Ambassador's residence for the reception.

Clustered in groups we waited for the Princess. Escorted by the Ambassador she moved from group to group. She met a large number of people. Her Lady in Waiting, Personal Secretary, her personal staff and all the members of the Queen's flight, well used to this sort of thing, were very easy and friendly guests. As the Princess stood among us, seeking to help the conversation my well rehearsed reference to us both being Benenden Seniors brought a rather surprising derogatory sniff.

The Princess left the party first, followed by the Ambassador. Razak brought the staff car and we headed off to Rawalpindi, like Cinderella going to the Ball. How the lights flashed, the sirens howled, and the Police saluted! The gates to the President's house were open and we swept in up the drive. President Zia ul Haq lived in a fine colonial bungalow with white pillared portico by the front door. We were invited to wait in the garden while the Princess was having an audience with the President inside. Soon the Princess came out with the President and his wife Begum Zia to meet us. Dinner was announced and the thirty guests were invited to go inside. In the hall were dozens of mementoes, plaques, photographs and presentations that had been made to the President. It was spacious but not palatial. The small dining room had been set out with three tables. The Princess sat next to the President at the top table. We sat at a round table next to the Foreign minister and the Governor of the North West Frontier Province. Zia's daughter was at our table too.

The talk ranged from the newly released film *Gandhi*, which had been forbidden in Pakistan, to national hockey and squash players and some very searching questions as to who our Pakistani friends were. After the meal the Princess and the President exchanged gifts. The Princess could be heard to say, as she handed over a signed photograph of herself, "Put that in your rogues gallery."

Then it was all over. We all left immediately. We drove out of the gates back into obscurity.

The evening was not over. Back in our house a splendid party was in progress...many weeks before we had invited the whole of the Queen's flight and the Princess's entourage to have dinner with us! We had organised a sit down candle-lit dinner for thirty six people! The substitute hosts we had had to appoint in our place had done very well....!

A Day in the Life....

6.00am   "This is the World Service of the BBC. Here is the news." So that's what is going on in Pakistan. The press, very strictly censored, kept the public conveniently ignorant of any disturbances in the country, and protests against the Zia administration in particular.

7.00am   Outside the heat haze hangs motionless over the hills. The parched garden lies breathless, the shrivelled leaves dry and dusty. The flowers await the baking sun. Another blazing day. Weeks and weeks of perfect weather.

"Good morning Aslam," I call as we come down for breakfast. The "Muslim" newspaper and the jug of orange juice await. The air conditioning thunders overhead, squeezing moisture into drips.

I must have a word with the staff.

"Had Abdul Rachmann come back from leave yet? I want to see him when he does."

He was two days late. What will the excuse be this time? He had used up 'My wife is ill,' and 'My roof is leaking,' and 'The bus was not running'....

"Maqbool, we are out tonight so we will have soup and cheese for lunch. Do we need anything from the market?"

7.45am   Colin leaves for work. I must attend to the accounts for the party the night before. I must write a letter to go in the 'Bag' today.

8.15am   Phone call from Colin. He will be bringing some businessmen home for lunch.

"Three more for lunch, Maqbool," I call. I shall certainly have to go to the market now.

9.30am   There is a hot blast as I go outside to the car. Perspiration sprouts on my forehead and trickles down my neck. Out in the sun the car becomes an oven. Lucky those with air conditioning in their cars! Hot air blows in and hot air blows out. Cotton clings and rivulets run down my back and legs.

Earlier birds than I have found the best places under the tree in the car park. Only a trace of shade is left. When the sun moves around the car will become a furnace.

I pass the refuse by the path. Do they ever clear it away? Huge crows pick and pull at it and the stench is disgusting. A group of men sit like sparrows on the wall. Dark eyes watch as I go by. They have nothing else to do all day. Somebody hawks.... somebody spits.... somebody else blows his nose through their fingers... How revolting! Just outside the market too!

Cool and dark inside I make my purchases. A fan lifts my skirt. A child watches me wide eyed. The mother glowers at me and turns away. "One kilo onions"... "Tomatoes good price".. The baskets fill up. Those poor chickens in their cages await a twist of their necks, and in a trice they are packed in a plastic bag... oven ready... "No chicken today."

11.00am   Outside the burning car awaits. On the way home I will call at the Thrift shop and then I'll go and see if Mahommet has come back from Murree. Perhaps he has finished my dress.

1.30pm   Home again. Aslam opens the door.

"Hallo Madam."

They are so polite!

"Aslam there are some baskets in the car, could you bring them out, and then bring me a LARGE orange juice?" The house is blissfully cool.... I collapse.

2.00pm   Colin arrives. Three car doors bang. They are here! I wonder who they are this time. The frigate lot again?

"Hallo darling, this is.... and here is the mail."

Introductions are made and a pile of letters are handed over. I long to sit down and read them but I must be polite to the guests.

3.30am   Lunch is over. I knew that I could leave everything to Maqbool. What a marvellous cook he is! The guests have gone, grateful to be spared a hotel meal and to be given a gin or whisky. I settle happily down with the mail.

4pm   Writing, phoning, planning, people to contact, things to do, but it is too hot. I'll stretch out in the sun. The staff have gone off duty. I'll go up on the top balcony.

4.45pm   That was long enough! Time for a shower before going off to play tennis.

5.00pm   Into tennis gear. Who are we playing with? and where? Are we on the German, Australian or the American Embassy Court?

Must not forget towels, and drink.

Sweat splashes into my eyes. It is a hard game! Whew! It's hot!

The sun sinks in a blaze of orange and pink, the midges bite. The evening birds wink and squawk. The clouds swell up over the hills into towering cream froths.

7.00pm   Time for a shower and a rest. Relax for an hour before we have to go out again. Where are we going? Check the invitations. A reception? A dinner? A Farewell? Oh well, there is time to lie down for a read. How I'd love an evening in!

The fans whirl as I get lost in my book. Colin snoozes. Aslam knocks on the door. We jerk awake.

"Razak is here Sahib," he calls.

Quick! we are late. What is the dress for tonight? Not dreaded uniform! It should be banned in the summer! What shall I wear! Oh dear they have seen this, and I wore that last time! Colin struggles into braces, tight trews, boots and straps. Fix on the braid. We are off.

The warm air enfolds us. The crickets chirrup. The glorious smells of the garden pervade all. What a lovely temperature. Decked out, we don the diplomatic cloak.

8.00pm   We arrive at the party, pretty lights are draped around the house, garden and the coloured shamianas (screens).

Razak drops us at the door.

"We won't be long Razak."

Up the red carpet past the candles lining the drive. Pin on the grin.

"Hallo how nice to see you".

We pass along the reception line. Photographers line up. Perhaps the President will attend. There are enough police outside. Drift off to a familiar face. Small talk... soft drinks... Where is the "Happy corner?" All the Begums crowd together into corners or onto the nearest chair. They say nothing. Sweet and smiling they are oh! so dull!....

The chatter goes on..."We haven't seen you for a long time".... "We didn't see you at...."... "When did you get back....?" What a lot of new faces.

Where is Colin, it's time to go on to the next party. Nobody queries late arrivals or early departures. We all have diplomatic ports of call.

11.00pm   Razak brings us home.

"Office time tomorrow Razak," says Colin. "Goodnight Abdul Rachmann you can shut the gate now."

"Goodnight sir."

The day is nearly done. Turn off the lights in the hall. The staff have gone to bed. The house is warm and comfortable. All is quiet. We go upstairs. It was a nice party and those new people were fun. The bed is turned down and blissfully cool. Another shower. It's not too late for a quick read.

It won't be like this at home will it?

Contented yawn.

Goodnight!

Lady of Leisure

Being relieved of household duties I looked elsewhere for activities to fill my time. I had been warned not to commit myself for at least three months so that I could see what was going on before deciding what to become involved with and what I wanted to support.

One day I was given a file and an invitation to tea at a Christian Children's Home in Rawalpindi. The owner of the file was indisposed and was returning to UK temporarily. By agreeing to go I had no idea what I was letting myself in for. I was instantly put on the committee and given the task of organising the big annual sale in Islamabad!

Gradually I was introduced to the charities to which the diplomatic community subscribe much of their time and funds. Working parties met weekly, making toys, cushions, knitting, sewing etc. All would be sold at the big St Joseph's Bazaar at Christmas. Veiled hints that I had a big house, that my predecessor had done it for a year, put me in a position for which I had neither answer nor excuse. I found that I had undertaken to run the Christmas Craft group every week in my house, I was certainly recruited by devious means!

I signed on at the Kindy and the Primary School, glad to help on a supply teaching basis when I could. I loved the Kindy. Blonde heads, golden heads, brown heads, there were children from all over the world. The Japanese children looked like little dolls with their beautiful porcelain skin, almond eyes and black fringed hair. The African children with their liquid black eyes and tightly curled eye lashes were angelic. They all played and painted together, though none angelic enough to resist bartering with the possessor of a coveted biscuit in the lunch break!

There were certainly no angels in the large class that I was asked to teach at the American International School. A multi-national, multi-coloured class of twenty six twelve year olds were consigned to my care for a few days. Though my experience had been with younger children I decided to give it a try.

Uncertain as to what was in store for me, I set off to school rather apprehensively. I would not only have a class that was older than I was accustomed to, but the children and the system would be unfamiliar as well. I consoled myself that there was an "aid" who would be able to work me in gradually....so I thought. The time I had to report was the same time as the children arrived in the school buses. I would not to have any time to look at the books before they came into class.

The aid bustled up to me full of advice. Her job was to help the teacher and do the odd jobs, mark books, make lists, plan visits to the library, escort the children to and from lessons elsewhere, in fact to do everything but teach. I hoped that she might hold the fort while I had a look to see what work the children were doing. It was not to be. I was in it up to my neck from the moment I walked in the door.

"You must do this," she said as a gigantic Maths book was pushed under my nose. "You'll have to ask them that," she said as she pointed out a page. "Don't forget to check that," she muttered. "You had better get started and introduce yourself, and don't forget the GRADES," she whispered darkly. She was obviously well practised in briefing new teachers.

"Could I do something of my own with them?" I asked weakly.

"No chance, they'll get behind," she said. "You must get on, it's time to start, and don't forget the GRADES."

Twenty six children sat there staring at me. They looked and were enormous! They waited expectantly for something to happen. I felt a rising panic as I realised that it was all up to me. I had never seen the Maths book before, I did not know what I was checking, what I had to mark, and I hadn't got a clue how to take the grades. I looked at the page and to my infinitesimal relief... it was something that I had taught before. Taking a deep breath I stepped in front of the class. I found myself telling them who I was with a confidence that I did not feel. Somehow I marked this, asked them that and I even managed to get some grades.

After Maths they split up into two groups. The 'aid' worked with one group of children in need of individual help. Others were working on assignments. I was to have a conference with the others asking them questions about something that I had not read, marking work that I had not set, and taking more grades. After English they all disappeared off to have music so I had a moment to think slowly....or so I thought. As she went out of the door the aid gave me a huge and very excellent book on Social Studies.

"Read this," she suggested. "Read these pages, it might be quite difficult. You will need time to think this out, it's quite hard, you will have to have a discussion with them about this and ask them questions about that. I think that you could have problems". She vanished out of the door before I had time to open my mouth.

My head hummed and my brain jammed solid as I read about the life style of South American Indians, their customs and their beliefs. I had to have examples ready to discuss on the beliefs and the rights and wrongs of different cultures. I had to give examples of beliefs based on fact and others on fiction. My pen scribbled frantically while I dredged up some ideas. There was no time for lunch as I gathered up my thoughts on these abstract subjects. The only saving grace was the fact that after the lesson they were to be shown a film strip and listen to a recording, which I presumed was to be shown by the aid in the very well equipped audio visual department.

Two minutes before the lesson a man appeared with a film projector and a record player, followed by the aid.

"What is this?" I asked shakily.

"You'll have to do it," said the aid. "You'll have to operate it yourself, and you will have to give them an introduction to the film as well."

I had twenty seconds before the children came in to learn how to operate the projector, and desperately read the notes on the film strip. I have to say that the aid was not at all what I had hoped for.

Not for the first time did I thank all those years of teaching experience. One does learn to extemporize! We had our discussions on the South American Indians, we had the film and the record, and suddenly... the day was done. I was still alive... Just...

"Any advice for tomorrow?" I asked the aid.

"Aw gee not at all," she grinned. "You've got no problems"...!

Whatever your interests hobbies or sports, there was ample opportunity to pursue them in Islamabad. We wasted no time in presenting ourselves on the tennis court, thrilled to have the time, climate, and people to play with. We must have played too much too soon. In a few weeks we were both suffering from tennis elbow. We felt in need of exercise, so we thought we would join the teeming throngs of golfers and see if we could fathom what induced such devotion. Just for such an event we had packed a set of antiquated golf clubs before we had left England. There were plenty of clubs for the two of us we thought. After all we only need one tennis racquet.

That all was not as it should be became apparent in the car park. No Mem hadn't got a bag. We gathered it was not quite Gleneagles to have only one bag between two players. Then came the problem of the balls and the ball boys. Before we knew where we were ten balls had been put in the pocket of the bag and another ten had been stuffed into the nether most regions of the all enveloping baggy trousers of the ball boys and caddies... For our requirements it seemed an excessive number of balls.

With an impressive escort of bag holders and ball boys we marched off to the launching pad. The tee was ceremoniously pinned in the ground, the ball perched on top and then we were invited to hit it.

The clubs are called irons or woods, a slightly unnecessary name since we could see that for ourselves. They were numbered up to thirteen. These I thought were very unimaginative names for clubs. How much better if they could be called wallopers or whackers, lifters, spoons, hookers or patters. At least I would have more idea what they were used for. How much more impressive to ask the caddy for a whacker, it has so much more colour and purpose to it.

A club about seven foot long was presented to me and I assumed the appropriate stance in front of the ball. I gathered it is called addressing the ball. I did not know I had to talk to it.

The ball looked microscopic... It was stationary after all. It couldn't be too difficult could it... It could... Just watch the ball and swing... A final look down the runway. Much golf is done by remote control it would appear. I could not see the green, the flag or the pole... There was a vast open space to hit into with no nets or lines to worry about... Watch the ball and swing... There was a shuddering thump as a clod of earth fell at my feet. Oh dear. What happened? The group of watchers drew closer. Don't lift your head, they said, follow through, watch the ball, don't watch the ball.

They were very kind to you when you were a beginner. The caddies retrieved the balls for me from six feet away or from the dandelion patch where they landed, always hopeful of better things.

We did leave the first tee eventually. Colin got into his stride and was cracking balls off in grand style, but for some reason he had a propensity for hitting things on the way. Balls ricocheted off telegraph poles, bounced off tree trunks, snapped off twigs and dived off into the undergrowth. We lost either two balls in six strokes or six balls in two strokes.

No matter how much we watched the ball, marked the place where it landed, tree, shrub or blade of grass and we walked to it, over it, into it or under it, the ball had vanished. Straight into the capacious trousers of the ball boys? We spent much time rummaging about in the rough. Our shoes and socks got covered in burrs and our legs in scratches as we took a closer look at the wild life. It was through the bushes that we realised that a formidable group of golfers was closing up behind. We would have to let them through. With unnecessary remarks like "What are you doing in the bushes?" and "No canoodling in there," they teed up, drove off and moved on, having effortlessly landed their ball on the invisible green three miles away.

Bunkers have been put in the direct line of fire to the green. They are tastefully arranged around the perimeter. I found that balls had a fascination for them and went out of their way to get in there, rolling carefully up to the brim and then dropping into the combed sand. Here I needed an ice cream scoop. More sand than ball came out. If the ball actually did rise to the top it trickled straight back in again.

At last I got onto the green. Carefully does it... just enough... and off the ball went. To the end it had a will of its own. It was up to all the tricks. It decided to have a look at the hole so it did a balancing trick as it circled the rim, coming to a halt a good safe distance away, or it made off with gay abandon to the gaping maw of another bunker.

Were we up to par? or down to par? As we staggered back to the club house the ball boys offered to sell our balls back to us. We talked about club fees, green fees, tee fees, caddy fees, and a set of clubs at Rs4000(200.00). Where did it all end? Well... we hoped that it would end back on the tennis court!

Life in Islamabad was nothing if not varied. Endless opportunities presented themselves. There was a very good amateur dramatic group called Rawalpindi Amateur Theatrical Society, (RATS). They put on excellent productions on stage at the International School, one of which was *The Pirates of Penzance*. Sir Oliver Forster, the British Ambassador, was the Modern 'Major General'. A talented aand enthusiastic actor he often took star parts in productions. Both Colin and I took part on stage. I was happier behind the scenes and enjoyed the makeup department sticking on beards and whiskers.

There was a lot of very professional talent in the British Embassy and it was given full reign. The Embassy pantomimes were hilarious. Play readings were popular and these we held in people's spacious homes or on the verandah or balconies on hot tropical nights. Our last production, *Blithe Spirit*, included in the cast three grandmothers!

As the months went by we became involved with musical activities. We put on two concerts at our house and finally two very big International ones in the Japanese Auditorium. We invited each country in the Attache Corps to put on a short entertainment typical of their country. These and other activities filled our days.... and nights. Also we entertained 1,434 people in our first six months! The heavy burden of entertaining was made easy by the staff, so we were determined to make the most of our time in Islamabad.

It was when we went out of town and explored the beautiful valleys that I began a hobby that I continued for many years afterwards. Because it provided a very real reminder of where we had been, I started to press flowers....

On getting an electric mixer mended...

Scene One - Electronic shop, Supermarket. Islamabad.

Me	Good morning, I am afraid that my mixer isn't working.
HIM	I see (Youth aged about 16 takes the mixer and stares at it).
ME	Could you mend it for me please?
	Inexpert hands begin to unscrew mixer. My confidence is not enhanced by his inability to find the screws in the first place. My mixer falls to pieces and becomes unrecognisable. Its entrails lie amongst a mass of other miscellaneous screws and wires. Hope fades that it will ever fit back into its nice clean cream coloured shell.
Me	What is the matter with it?
HIM	Ek minute (further experiments). You come back tomorrow please my brother come.
ME	(Relieved that there was an elder brother). Can it be mended or not?
HIM	My brother come.
EXIT	

Scene Two. Next day, same place.

ME	How are you getting on, did your brother come?
HIM	My brother come tomorrow.
ME	Look! I need my machine, where is your brother?
HIM	Him come tomorrow.
	I spot my machine in a dusty corner together with the innards of a TV set and a cathode tube.
ME	Can somebody else look at it...another person?
HIM	Brother come, you wait...
ME	I can't wait, and I need my machine... I have a big party very soon...
HIM	OK... Please sit down...
ME	Would you please tell your brother that I need my mixer as soon as possible. I must have it...
HIM	You want tea?..

ME   No I don't want tea, I want my mixer. PLEASE TELL YOUR BROTHER.

EXIT

Scene Three. The same. Five days later.

An apprehensive smile flutters across his face as he spots me.

ME   Has your brother looked at my mixer yet? You have had it for five days now. Where is your brother?

Mixer is unearthed from behind heaps of old radios and calculators. I hardly recognise it. It actually is back in its shell but overlaid with thick layers of black greasy finger marks.

HIM   You wait ek minute.

ME   (Fuming) Is your brother here?

HIM   My grandfather, grandmother, cousin all die, brother not come.

ME   Did you mend it?

HIM   Machine no good. My brother come.

I was quite unable to work this one out, but thankfully at that moment in walked brother.

ME   Salaam ale cum. Have you been able to mend my mixer for me?

As if from a great distance he focussed on me and clicked his fingers to his younger brother. The mixer was handed over. With great deliberation and exasperatingly slowly he began to unscrew it. Like a surgeon, orders were given for spanners, tweezers, oil, plugs, wires, all of which were lined up and used for probing the intestines of my machine. Like cracking a nut open, the machine fell to bits. Ten minutes later the pathologist had completed his examination.

BROTHER This machine is no good...

ME   (Getting frantic at the snail's pace that everything was being conducted) What is wrong with it? Can you mend it?

BROTHER Sit down please. You want tea?

ME   No thank you, I don't want any tea, and I am in a terrible hurry, I have a very big party today and I must have a mixer.

The offending part of the mixer is pointed out to me.

BROTHER That no good. New part needed. No have here. Sorry, no mend.

ME   So the machine is finished?

BROTHER Yes please, Sorry.

We Give A Party

The time had come when we felt that we must start doing some entertaining. We had practised with the staff on small informal dinner parties and we now felt confident to launch ourselves on a larger scale. It was friends in the Corps of Service Attaches that we invited to our first big party. We wanted to repay them for the kindly welcome that they had given us when we first arrived. Since so many official functions brought us together we felt that we would like to try something informal. We would have a Games Party.

Those to whom we mentioned it sucked their teeth and told us that it would not work. It would be fraught with difficulties. For a start they said many would not answer the invitation. Some will tell you that they are coming and then not turn up. Others that accept will not come, those that decline will arrive. They wished us luck but they made it clear that they thought the whole thing could well be a disaster. We knew that the shy gentle Asian ladies smile and say little, and that others find it difficult to remain upright for longer than it takes to find the nearest chair. We wondered if they would join in.

As time went on the party drew closer. We began to plan the party in detail. Four teams would progress to different activities and games. Later would come passing a matchbox on noses down the team and other absurdities.

"The Moslems won't like that," said somebody.

"You won't get them doing that," said somebody else.

"Just you wait and see," we said gritting our teeth.

A turkey was bought and instructions were given to Maqbool. "Make sure you cook it the day before," I told him.

I had no qualms. He was one of the best cooks in Islamabad. He had prepared dozens of parties.

All went well until two days before the party. As we had been warned, and had secretly feared, the telephone rang. It was "Burma" to say that he had to attend a dinner at his Ambassador's house. Next came a call from "Malaysia" saying that he had to attend to pressing business elsewhere. Then came calls from Thailand, Indonesia and China, all of whom had left it until the last minute before making up their minds whether to come or not. None of them would come. A growing feeling of unease came over us. Had they taken fright at the thought of having fun and games? Were the predictions right?

The day dawned without further cancellations until lunch time, when France rang to say that his wife would not be accompanying him. At lunch time I went into the kitchen to check how the preparations were going. To my dismay there sitting on the table in its original naked state was my 20lb turkey. It was unstuffed, uncooked and unready.

"Maqbool put that thing in the oven," I cried. "You'll never have it ready in time."

At 5 o'clock the telephone rang again. An American voice drawled, "Do we eat at your place?" she said. Most Americans eat at 7 o'clock. The invitation had not specified dinner though a party at 8pm at home would automatically include a meal. In our ignorance we assumed that everybody would know this. We were very unwise to assume anything in the diplomatic life. A hideous doubt crept into our minds. How many other people ate at 7 o'clock, or five o'clock or 6 o'clock? There was nothing else for it but to ring up everybody and tell them.

Our final list included Attaches from France, Germany, Australia, Ghana, Jordan, Egypt, India, Somalia, United States and Japan.

At 7 o'clock I went into the kitchen. It was crawling like an ants' nest with a seething mass of cooks and bearers, most of whom I had never seen before. They had all been summoned by Maqbool to help. There on the table was my turkey. Beside it, all I could see over the top of the table was a pair of bright beady eyes gleaming over a huge twitching moustache. The owner of the whiskers was attacking my turkey with a gigantic carving knife. Pieces of turkey flew like confetti as large and small lumps of meat fell higgledy piggledy all over a stone cold plate. The stuffing was being sprinkled in handfuls, while the tomato baskets were sitting cold and forlorn far removed from their intended destination.

Maqbool commanded his troops. No doubt it was quite clear in his mind what he was doing. It was also quite clear that what was in his mind had not been in mine. Maybe he had understood, maybe not. More than likely he had decided to do the simplest thing which was to do what he had done before. I made up my mind to show him exactly what I wanted the next time. It was too late now. There was nothing else for it but to beat a retreat before I was trampled under foot. I backed out of the kitchen with a sigh. The Unions had taken over and the shop floor was in control. If I had tried to redeem the situation it was quite clear that nobody would stop to listen. This was no place for the Mem.

By now the guests had begun to arrive. Soon it became a guessing game as to who was coming or who was not. Wives that were not expected arrived. Malaysia who had declined walked in the door. Egypt arrived just as we were about to go into dinner. Ghana came for a few minutes just enough time to have dinner and then disappeared to go to the airport to meet his wife, which was a revelation to us since she was supposed to be sitting down to have dinner with us! Jordan and Somalia did not turn up at all. After the fourth attempt to rearrange the table plan while the guests were arriving, in desperation we dropped all the place names into the wastepaper basket. They could sit anywhere. We had lost track of who we had, who was coming, who was lost, and who had gone. They seemed to be having their own brand of fun and games.

Luckily the rest of the party was a huge success. We had the Begums crawling on the floor, and waving their arms about, and laughing their heads off as matchboxes were passed along the rows on noses. The Ghanaian (who had returned) complained loudly that it was most unfair to use western matchboxes since they were not designed for African noses!

The staff, watching the hilarity, peeped around the doorways. It was not long before they had started cheering on the teams as they played golf on the hall carpet. My midget of turkey fame quite forgot himself and started cheering and yelling instructions until finally he could contain himself no longer and gave a demonstration to all and sundry how to score a putt.

By general agreement it was voted a great success, we had kept the Begums upright and they had not laughed so much in years. We had had our hair-raising moments and our critics had been proved correct, but it also proved the point that people from all over the world can laugh at themselves...and find silly games fun.

The Jumma Bazaar

Hustle bustle, hurry on
Take your bundles and your bags.
All is cheap and bargains wait
Bursting baskets, bulging bales
Willing hands and straining arms
Lifting, tipping, heaving
Onto stall, cart or sack.
Come barter, pick, the choice is yours.
Prod and squeeze
How much is that, and this?
Crouching, sitting eager men
Sorting, sifting, patting piles
Swift with scales and deft with weights,
Watching as the Mem goes by.

Mangoes, melons, trays of dates
Oranges, lemons, seedless grapes,
Garlic bulbs, banana hands
Carrots, onions, cabbage too.
Nameless spices, biscuits, tea,
Soap in piles and nuts in bags
Stalls of gaudy plastic bowls
Shoddy shoes and useless toys
Dishes, pots in shiny tin
Quick to burn and hot to hold.

Pointing fingers, darting eyes
Watching as the Mem goes by.
On stalls and tables, bamboo poles
Hang children's clothes and bras so bold.
Screens of cotton, coloured cloth
Faceless women, shrouded, veiled
Picking over grubby lengths
Like sifting dirty laundry piles.
A sideways look,

A whispered word,
Watching as the Mem goes by.

Pewter-coloured heavy bangles
Dangle earrings, ornate beads,
Crude to wear but cheap to buy.
Inlaid boxes set with stones
Mid Afghan carpets by the road
Brought from distant village hearth
By grey eyed merchants,
Watching as the Mem goes by.

Mid stench and squawks,
Battered, broken birds
Caged and condemned,
Await their death
By heartless humans bent on greed.
A twist of neck
A life has gone
The Mem cannot look as she goes by.

The Great Trunk Road to Peshawar

The Pakistan Services plan tours for the Corps of Service Attaches to cities such as Karachi, Lahore and Peshawar. Colin's father had served in Peshawar, and his brother had been born there, so when we were invited to join the Peshawar tour, to attend a wedding, and to drive up the Khyber Pass, we were delighted to have the opportunity to explore some of the places of Colin's childhood.

Islamabad with its modern buildings, clean streets, and tree-lined avenues was very different from the scene that greeted us as we joined the traffic on the Great Trunk road. Here we had our first glimpse of the poor and primitive conditions that people lived in in the villages. Shops with their black and greasy doorways consisted of little more than piled up crates and boxes, shelter provided by sacking or tarpaulin propped up on poles. Life was conducted by the roadside. Dogs and children played in the dust that swirled up as we passed. Men lay on charpoys in the shade, roadside stalls sold bottled drinks and coloured sweets. Hygiene was of the most primitive. I could only imagine the contamination of food by dust, flies and mosquitoes that swarmed over the fruit, vegetable and meat stalls.

In the towns and villages men wandered along the road, some holding hands, others greeting each other with unselfconscious embraces. They seemed to have nothing to do. There was little for them to do. There were no cinemas, theatres, no amusements. Their only means of passing the time was playing games of dice or kicking a football, or playing cricket on the dusty verges. Shopkeepers were mending furniture, cars, machines, or making clothes.

Donkeys plodded along the road carrying their burdens of bricks, stones, baskets, bales, or people. Little hummocks of grass trotted along the road, a pair of human legs just visible underneath. Buses and lorries hurtled down the road giving no heed to man nor beast, their human attachments clinging on like limpets. We saw some poor buffaloes jammed tight in the back of a lorry tied tightly by the nose to the rails cushioning each other as they sped along. Barely able to turn their heads, we could just see their terrified eyes.

There had been many brave British soldiers that had left their name and fame behind them. We passed a monument to one of them. His name was General John Nicholson. He had been a folk hero of Victorian Britain. His story typifies the brave and the best that were sent to India during the last century.

John Nicholson, tough, proud and determined, was an ideal man to bring law and order to the tribes of the Frontier. In 1852 he was sent to Bannu, a district near Peshawar to bring to heel the Wazir tribe, who were defying British authority. It took him six months to succeed. Ruthless and unshrinking

A Pakistani village

in carrying out his duty he could be as blood thirsty as they. The floggings and hangings that he meted out as punishments finally brought the Wazirs under control. He personally sliced off the head of a highwayman which he kept on his desk as a warning! The Pathans had met their match. Though hated and feared by some, there were others who loved and respected him. A sect called Nickel Seyn literally worshipped him.

In 1857 after the start of the Indian Mutiny, uprisings in the Frontier had to be dealt with swiftly to prevent trouble spreading. It was vitally important to separate any potentially mutinous regiments and to deal firmly with skirmishes as they happened. In Nowshera an uprising was brewing. Nicholson spotted 500 insurgents close to Mardan and he personally gave chase and flushed them out of their hiding places amongst the crags of the Malakand Pass. Two hundred sepoys were killed and one hundred and twenty were wounded. Nicholson personally accounted for a good many.

Back in Peshawar vengeance was pitiless. Forty were sentenced to death. In chains and shaking with terror, watched by the assembled garrison and thousands of Pathans, they were blown from the mouths of cannons.

In 1857 Nicholson was sent to Delhi as a Brigadier General, aged thirty four, to spearhead the assault on the walls of the city. In the thick of the battle whilst rallying his men, he was finally killed by a shot through his lung. A brave and fearless man, he was the right man in the right place at the right time.

Further up the road was Taxila, a town that has become the scene of fascinating archaeological finds. The adventurers of old found the fertile valley very much to their liking, and it became over the centuries a meeting place for the trade routes connecting China, India, Asia and the West.

Empires succeeded each other during the centuries between 600 BC and 600 AD. Alexander the Great and the Bacterian Greeks established their capital there. In 60 AD the Kushans from Central Asia flowed in bringing Buddhism and the Gandharan civilization. These ancient cultures overlaid and buried each other during the succeeding centuries until more recently archaeological experts began to uncover a profusion of treasures that revealed the secrets of those far-off times. They are of such quality and variety they are now in museums and private collections all over the world.

We passed the Tarbela Dam. We were amazed at the sheer endeavour that has created the largest earth-filled dam in the world. It also has the largest electricity generating power and the biggest spillways in the world. The mighty Indus had been dammed to provide much needed irrigation water and electric power.

We passed the grim sinister fort of Attock, below which the blue water of the Indus flows beside the brown waters of the Kabul river.

We neared Peshawar and drove through the military town of Nowshera, the home of the Armoured Corps. On either side we could see the old Raj style bungalows standing back from the road. The pale yellow wash on the walls now faded and flaking. A verandah ran around the houses under arches, and the tiny windows were set high up in the walls. Bungalows like these had housed the British in their cantonments all over India.

A Raj style bungalow

The Regiments stationed here had the job of safeguarding the North West Frontier Province. The barracks was well kept. Even the pot plants were painted and on parade in straight lines. Soldiers in their puggarees were being instructed on weapon practice, while on the hockey field a match was in progress. The British had left, but little else had changed. There were Quarter master's stores, Officers' Messes, and an Instruction Hall; our Armoured Corps family and friends would feel very much at home.

The few women we saw were much more retiring than their Islamabad counterparts. They were wearing the all-enveloping "Bourka". The full length cotton cloak fitted to the head and falling in gathers to the ground. The world was only visible through small holes in front of their eyes. In full blast of summer women must have to contend with a heat that defies imagination.

From the age of puberty, girls are secluded from the outside world. In the villages from an early age girls are expected to work in the fields tending the animals, collecting the manure for fuel, and helping their mothers with the chores and the younger children.

It is possible that until she is married she may well not see any man except her father, brothers or relatives. Finding a husband is of prime importance to her family. The marriage is arranged by both sets of parents. Once she is married she lives with her husband's family and is expected to look after the home, and provide a son.

Tremendous national efforts are under way to enlighten and educate the rural female population, but it will take generations to change the attitudes of simple women and more importantly the men. It is they who wish to keep their women shut up at home and see no reason to educate them. Tribal ancestors have passed on traditional customs and religious constraints that have remained unchanged for centuries.

Women have a hard life; seen without the "Bourka" their faces reflected the life they led. Their skins were lined and creased like leather and they looked old before their time. They had a hard uncompromising look in their eyes and stoic acceptance of a life that held little in the way of comforts or consideration. Any youthful refinement or femininity had been overlaid by marriage, childbearing and hard work. There was a world of difference between their articulate, sophisticated and beautifully groomed sisters in Islamabad.

The traffic intensified as we neared Peshawar and we joined the carts and bicycles and the busy bustle. Little Vespa motorised rickshaws scooted in and out of the traffic. For the cost of a rupee or two it must be the cheapest and the coolest way for their passengers to explore the sights and sniff the smells as they burrow their way through the bazaars.

On the roadside were some of the poorest homes. Grubby little children were playing in the dirt under some twigs and a few wisps of cloth that hardly provided shelter or shade. There were the barest essentials for surviving among the rags. Exposed to the sun in the summer, heaven knows how they survived the torrential rain when it came.

In sharp contrast was the Balahissar Fort. A huge impregnable mass of brick and stone. A menacing place used either to keep people in or to keep them out. Babur, a descendant of Tamerlane the Turk and Ghenghis Khan, built the fort in the 16th century. It was destroyed by the Sikhs in 1818 when they captured Peshawar. In 1849 the British took Peshawar from the Sikhs and rebuilt the fort. It was needed as a stockade to conduct their endless campaigns against the warring tribes in the North West Frontier. It was now the HQ of the Frontier Corps, a military force of 40,000 men.

We entered the cantonment to shady avenues and quiet residential roads. Here too were the Government Offices, military camps, police headquarters, museums and Universities, and the place where we were going to stay. The Khyber Intercontinental Hotel.

The Pakistani Highway Code

1. Drive as fast as you can, especially in crowded areas.
2. Overtake on corners, crossroads, roundabouts and narrow roads.
3. Pull out of side roads or parking areas in front of other cars.
4. Always scatter pedestrians by giving them a blast on the horn.
5. Make as much noise as you can when there are goats, cows or other animals about.
6. Ease the approaching traffic onto the verge.
7. Get as many people as possible in your car, taxi, lorry or bus. If there is no room inside pile them up on the roof.
8. Load your truck as high as you can with heavy items.
9. Park as close as possible in front of other cars.
10. Wet conditions are ideal for speeding.
11. Take hash before driving, especially before you drive up the mountain passes.
12. Push in when you like at roundabouts.
13. If you are stopped by the police, bribe them.
14. Never report an accident. It will be blamed on you.
15. Pedestrians never look before you cross the road.
16. Use your horn day and night in residential areas.
17. Park your car on corners and bridges.
18. Stop suddenly. Do not indicate what you are going to do.
19. Cyclists do not need lights at night.

We Are Invited to a Wedding

The Khyber Intercontinental Hotel has an impressive appearance and setting. Flags and flowerbeds and a sweeping drive lulled us into thinking that we were to be cocooned in five star comfort. We have reason to believe that after the following episode happened the management of the Khyber Intercontinental changed and those people that stayed there subsequently were more than satisfied with the service and the rooms. We were unlucky to have been there at the time the hotel was going through a bad patch.

We arrived at the entrance and went through the swing doors past the man with his smart uniform, plumes, puggarees and red beard. The striking red hair, and beards that are seen are the symbols of the "Haj" pilgrimage to Mecca, that devout Moslems hope to make once in their life times.

We signed on at the reception desk and were assigned rooms on the second floor. Silently we trod the carpeted corridors to our boudoir. The room looked very small and crowded with furniture. Puce, pink and orange screamed at us and there came forth a dingy smell. Dirty wipe marks graced the bathroom. The floors were unhoovered and unbrushed, other peoples threads and crumbs were pressed into the pile carpet and the bedspreads were stained. Hardly visible behind the heavy curtains, were grimy lace drapes that were indescribably dirty. Fly marks, dust and filth were so ingrained that the curtains were all locked onto their runners.

Colin called the manager who tried to sweep the bedspreads off with one hand and wipe the bathroom with the other.

"Find us another room!" Colin bellowed. "How can you let your guests stay in such a filthy room?"

"You are right," he wailed. "No good, no good. I find another room this minute."

... A few minutes later the door opened to an abjectly anguished floor manager.

"We have a good room, you come please." Leading the way he fussed and apologised down the passage.

We were invited to look at the new room. We did a tour of inspection. Swift work had been done in there. The bathroom floor was suspiciously damp and what looked like extremely new bedspreads had been put on the beds. A glance into the cupboard revealed the old ones had been screwed up and flung into the corner. The lace curtains were one degree cleaner.

Suitcases were brought in and were dumped...upside down. Like a stage play another player came in, this time carrying a basket of fruit and biscuits. A cloth was produced with a flourish and laid on the table and the basket of fruit was placed as a centre piece.

Yet another manager appeared with a pot of flowers. I was beginning to have grave difficulty stifling the giggles. With a bow they backed off stage.

The door opened again. It was another, even more senior, Manager. "I have a good room for you on the fourth floor with a reception room for the same price."

We were not keen to move again, but their concern had atoned somewhat for the hotel's shortcomings.

"Come with me," the Manager entreated.

Into the lift we went. With a confident flourish the Manager pushed the button to take us up to the fourth floor. Twenty seconds later the door opened. He had pushed the wrong button! Instead of arriving at the fourth floor....we had descended..... to ground level!

We had been invited to a Moslem wedding in the hotel. We watched the bride arrive at the front door in a car that was completely covered in strands of tinsel from bonnet to boot. She was escorted by her attendants of female members of her family. She looked very beautiful in her gown of pale green chiffon, heavily embroidered in gold and sequins. She walked into the foyer and then into the lift. There was no way that Colin and I were to share the celebrations. He was sent one way and I was sent in another.

In an upstairs room the bride entered an enormous reception room flanked on three sides by hundreds of women sitting in rows facing inwards. At the far end was a dais brightly lit and heavily decorated by tinsel and dangles. Several easy chairs awaited the arrival of the bride. She took her place in the centre with her attendants around her and was shortly the centre of attraction. A long queue of friends and well wishers came to talk to her and take photographs.

Timidly I asked another guest standing by the door what I was supposed to do. In a perfunctory manner I was waved away and told to sit somewhere. There seemed to be no hostess to whom I could make myself known. Thankfully I found a seat at the back where I could watch without being observed.

There were no bourkas here. There were no hidden women and no veils. They were all beautifully dressed in gorgeous saris and shalwar chemis. The colours were breathtaking. There were silks and satins in purples, pinks, brilliant greens, royal blues, scarlet and orange. Gold and silver embroidery was lavished everywhere. The edges, collars, cuffs, jackets and hems were all encrusted to wonderful effect. Their clothes were matched by exquisite jewellery in their ears, necks and wrists. Highly ornamental dangles and chains with every colour of stone hung in rows that glittered and glowed. In their hair they had flowers and ribbons threaded with gold and silver. These were the beautiful elegant women of Pakistan. It was obvious that I was the only European there.

Beside these gorgeous creatures were a whole host of assorted junior attachments that sucked their fingers, bottles or sweetmeats administered by outsize ayas who sprawled over their seats and overflowed others. Occasional cuffs and spanks and reprimands were given in a vain attempt to discipline the small fry who were determined to enjoy the party.

There was a movement towards one end of the room which gradually swelled to a huge tide. It was time for food. By the time the seething torrent had reached the tables the place was unrecognisable. Women were pushing and shoving and grabbing the food, stretching over their neighbours, spooning food onto plates and almost over each other. Carried along by the tide I found myself against the table. I picked up a plate and handed it to my neighbour who snatched it out of my hand. I was horrified to see that they shovelled in handfuls of meat and gravy with chappati held in their diamond encrusted nail varnished fingers. It was an incredible sight and one which I did not greatly enjoy. My beautiful butterflies had turned into locusts!

An untidy heap of plates announced that the business of eating was over and chatter could resume. The bride still sat where she was on her dais. I hoped that she had been given some food.

I was beginning to wonder when the wedding was to start. Where was the bridegroom? Was there to be a procession? Service? Music? I decided to find out.

"What happens now?" I ventured to ask one woman who had stopped talking briefly to draw breath.

"Go home of course," she told me in a pitying sort of way.

Realising that there was little to be gained by staying there I trailed away, hoping to find Colin. Since I did not know who the bride's mother was or even the bride and that nobody would notice if I was there or not I slipped away. I found Colin in the hall. His evening had followed the same pattern as mine. He had not even discovered who the bridegroom was.

Subsequently we discovered that the party we had been invited to had been a reception given by the bridegroom's father after the wedding. The bride had been the granddaughter of the late President of Pakistan, Ayub Khan.

Attache Wives Tour

It was from the Intercontinental Hotel that we set off for the first part of the Corps of Service Attache's tour. We began our programme at the Pakistan Air Force base. Brand new and still under construction, the new Cadets' Mess was an imposing sight. From it we could see new recruits on the parade ground, so new they had yet to be issued with their uniforms. The ladies were photographed on the spot where Mahommed Ali Jinnah, the first President of Pakistan took a parade, and by the war memorial. My request to take my own pictures was predictably refused. We were shown a very lovely display of national costumes by the wives on the station, and a selection of embroidery and weaving made by soldiers' wives who were under instruction. We were most charmingly entertained by the Officers in their Mess, who were courteous and delightful hosts.

The next day another plan had been made for us and to Nowshera we were taken to spend the morning there. We saw the ante-natal clinic, that looked little more than a bare whitewashed room with hard chairs around the edge. Since women in Pakistan will not allow a man to attend them women doctors were much in demand.

In another room wives were being instructed how to sew and embroider mats, towels, dresses and table cloths. When they have acquired the necessary skill they were then qualified to go out and earn money as seamstresses or dressmakers. Their work was laid out and we were invited to choose what we would like. Many of us left with beautiful bedspreads that we with difficulty had insisted that we paid for.

It was warm and we stopped for breaks under the open coloured tents and screens called shamianas on our morning tour. Easy chairs had been set out around the edge with carpets on the grass. At the far end sitting in rows, in perfect silence were about twenty five soldiers' wives watching us and every movement. Nobody spoke. Any smiles in their direction were greeted by stony stares or peals of girlish giggles. There was no encouragement on the part of our hosts for us to go and talk to them or to tell them how much we had admired their handiwork. I was unhappy that we should have been segregated and we were only allowed to smile at them from a distance.

There was more handiwork to admire, this time done by the children. My request to film the proceedings was greeted with much concern. My insistence that there could be nothing about a children's handiwork stall that could compromise the national security eventually won a grudging agreement.

The camp bakery was the final call of the morning. There, in spotless conditions, chappatis and biscuits were being turned out on a conveyer belt. It was here that we were presented with a cake iced and decorated, made by the bakers.

They had not finished with us yet. In an adjoining garden by a small lake, an enormous feast had been laid out. Under the shamianas piles of patties, cookies, cream cakes and sandwiches, salads, meats and sticky orange pretzels. Glancing at my watch I found that we were within ten minutes of joining our husbands for lunch. Not for the first time I admired the stamina of those amongst us that had a limitless capacity for eating and drinking anything, anywhere at any time. They were already munching away. I had to admit defeat. A polite nibble was all I could manage before we were finally driven to the imposing Armoured Corps Mess. My lovely cake and I were beginning to feel and look the same, melting on the top and dripping down the sides. It was with relief that we collapsed into comfortable chairs in the wonderfully cool and airy ante room.

A display of national dancing on the lawn brought our commitment with the military to an end. Back at the car I discovered that my poor cake had shed its coat of sugar altogether and was sitting in a mush in its box. It had been a long hot morning for both of us.

The Attache tour had been the first opportunity for us to meet and see many different Pakistani women. We had seen the village women, I had seen the elegant emancipated ones at the wedding. We had met officers and soldiers' wives, teachers and doctors as we went around. Those to whom we had spoken were happy to talk to us, or to tell us about their work, but they lost their confidence and identity when in the company of men.

We were invited to the Pakistan Air Force Mess in Peshawar. As in all the Messes there were the usual plaques, mementoes, portraits and silver. It was built by the British and similar to any mess one might go into in UK.

Our hosts were charming and we were most graciously received in the hall. Being unaware then of the social conventions I was surprised to see in an adjoining room, all the ladies. Those in the line ahead of us made their way with unerring step to join them. What are they going in there for I wondered? All around the room, on easy chairs the Begums sat in total silence. Unsure as to what I was supposed to do but seeing that some of the American and Australian wives were staying with their husbands I did likewise.

Ten minutes later one of the senior officers to whom I was talking asked me if I would like to meet his wife. Unable to refuse the hint that my presence was preferred elsewhere, I followed him into the hall of Begums. It was all very quiet. A few minutes later, after the strain of making one sided conversation began to take its toll, I invited my neighbour to come and meet my husband. Would she brave the vast concourse of men outside? Like me she had no alternative. I led her outside and introduced her to Colin. I knew it could not last. My companion had already disappeared when another officer came up and suggested that I would be more comfortable in the other room. I noticed that before long the other wives who had made a bid for freedom had also been ushered into the silent fold.

This segregation of men and women at all social occasions was something that I found very hard to accept all the time I was in Pakistan. There seemed to be no obligation or desire on the part of either men or women that they should have any social interchange at parties.

I could appreciate their reluctance to talk to me but I could not understand their reluctance to talk to each other.

The Wizards of Waziristan

The Salt Range,
A tame name for a wilderness
Of huge cliffs like a giant layer cake
Angled to the sky.
Of mountain ridges
With sharpened teeth
To snap and bite.
A wizard's kingdom
Of carved rock and stone.
Buttresses, caves and cavities,
Attics in the air,
A lair for bat or raven,
A hideout in the crags.
Thrown up, eroded into
A fossilized citadel
Of rocky ramparts.
Wild and weird lie
Misshapen humps like sleeping dinosaurs,
Rock and stone for claws and head.
An ossified guardians of
The Wizards of Waziristan
Await a wand
To come to life.

The Bazaars in Peshawar

There can be no place that evokes the true flavour of a country more effectively than its bazaars. There in amongst the alleyways and alcoves lies the heart, soul, life and history of the city. There walk the living testaments of the past. The descendants of the people that swarmed over the passes from Greece, Persia, Tibet, and China for reasons of explorations or expansion, plunder or peace. The old Buddhists and Moghuls of the past, all of whom moved on or died out, left cultures and traces of their facial features on the faces of those who now live at this crossroads of the world.

Here are the fierce Pathans, the fighting Afridis, the merchants from Afghanistan, the slant-eyed Chinese and Tibetans, Punjabis, Sindis, Baluchis and the tribes people that come from the mountains of Chitral, Gilgit, Hunza and Swat. They come to buy, sell, seek fortunes and favours, or to while away the endless hours on chair or charpoy.

A concentrated conglomeration of assorted headgear shuffled and shambled amongst the cotton clad crowds. Every conceivable variation of scarf winding could be seen. Scarves, cloth and strips of rag were twirled up and perched on top or wound and tied in knots. There were hats and turbans and Baluchi and Sindi caps, and others in gold or crochet work. The headgear was as varied as the faces that wore them. The dark-skinned multitudes seethed and milled about vying with the traffic, the carts, the donkeys and the bullocks for room on the road and a passage in the mainstream.

Down the alleyways, courtyards and in the market places sat the merchants cross-legged by their wares. They were selling soap and spices, tin and tea, carpets and cloth, fruit and fried food, copper and jewellery and bangles and baubles. Everything awaited our custom. Money lenders were perched on ledges like sparrows with their well-worn wooden bowls for cash. There were men sitting on mats in the middle of the market square having their heads shaved, their whiskers removed, their shoes cleaned or their teeth taken out. There were stalls of food with their attendant veils of flies by the open drains. Refuse in piles deterred not the unseeing throngs. Somebody wandered by with a parrot in a cage, another with hens in baskets. A woman passed with a sewing machine on her head. Donkeys and goats ambled in and out of the traffic and women in bourkas glided about clutching children and purses. They hurried out of sight as we stared.

In every direction there were inviting looking wares. An alcove selling materials resembled an Aladdin's cave. Piled up bales and hanging in curtains and swathes were the chiffons, silks and gossamer nets and tulle. Purples, pinks, puce and brilliant emeralds, scarlets, yellows and blues, all embroidered with threads of gold and silver were a riot of colour. Sitting in their alcoves waiting like spiders to trap us, the merchants watched us speculatively hoping we might be enticed into their web.

From Afghanistan boxes inlaid with lapis lazuli and jade lay among dusty bangles, medals and coins. Smells of frying emanated from dark corners. Old men sat crouching on steps earnestly discussing trade or transactions, others were stretched out sleeping on the floor or cushions.

We were interested in looking for pieces of Gandhara sculpture that we had heard could be found in the bazaars of Peshawar. Now a rarity and regarded as national heirlooms, the genuine articles were hard to find. There were fakes a-plenty which defy identification even by the experts, so for us it would be impossible to distinguish the authentic from the counterfeit.

We made enquiries at a likely shop that had dusty old stones and ancient carvings under a cracked glass counter; within seconds from amongst the attendant gawping crowds who gathered around any potential purchaser, came forth a toothless old man who then assumed the role of guide. Silently he beckoned us to follow him. He then proceeded to lead us down the alley way looking behind us to see if we were following him. He led up some steps opening to an inner courtyard surrounded by a network of attics. A slimy green water trough dripped into an open drain and pungent odours emanated from a dingy hole in the wall.

It was obviously tea time, as the carriers of blue enamel teapots were going about their business delivering trays to traders waiting within their lairs. We were led through dusty curtains into an inner sanctum, its walls covered in heavy metal necklaces and pewter bangles. Quick words were exchanged and we were taken to an even smaller room, just big enough for three people. Here in a recess was a safe. It looked interesting and promising. The curtain was pulled behind us. This must be where the genuine article was to be found. Paper bags and plastic bags were undone and their contents were tipped out on the table. Here were the little Gandharan heads we had been looking for. If genuine, they had come from the stone murals that had adorned the temples during the Gandharan civilization. Gandharan art represents a merging of the Greek, Persian, Syrian and Indian art traditions, and is renowned for the delicate detail depicted in the graceful swathes and drapes of a robe, or the detail of facial features. The little heads before us may or may not have been part of the frieze from former days, but the secrecy surrounding their exposure led us to believe they could have been. Half an hour later after bargaining against what they insisted were genuine prices, we left....having paid exactly half.

Waiting outside was our guide.

"You want more?" he asked.

"No thank you, enough." We told him.

He was not to be deterred.

"OK you come, no buy," he insisted.

This time we were led down what was little more than a crack in the wall. We could touch the grimy walls on each side as we passed. Through an opening with broken boards that passed as a door, down a dimly lit passage full of rubble we went. Would we be lost for ever in the myriad of mouse holes that ran like tunnels in the back streets? If our guide left us we doubted if we would ever see the light of day again.

We followed him blindly up some steps that looked as precarious as matchwood. Up a stairway so narrow our shoulders touched the walls on either side, we crept in semi-darkness. Our feet slipped through cracks in the floorboards that creaked as we passed. Finally we reached a doorway. Dimly we saw we were in an attic, and on the floor a huge pile of rubble had been tipped out. We were invited to sit on the floor and pick over the pieces of pottery. It was obviously a recent consignment from some archaeological excavation. The inaccessibility of the hiding place lent authenticity to the collection. From nowhere a strange assortment of shawled shapes had collected and five pairs of beady eyes were watching from the door.

The prices were absurd. They knew it and we knew it. There was to be no converging to a mutual agreement. We turned to go downstairs again.

"What is your best price?" they entreated, dismayed to find their prey escaping.

"We've said our best price, no more," we said firmly.

We marched down the stairs again followed by the shuffling shapes, and the guide who saw his commission disappearing out of the window. At the bottom of the steps we emerged into daylight again. The shapes now brought themselves into the discussion as we walked down the alley.

"No more, no more," we said, shaking our heads.

"Finish..OK," they said. "You have pieces, wait here." They scurried back up the passage and up to the attic again.

Three minutes later the heads we had discussed appeared in a paper bag, and exchanged for the price we had quoted all along.

We had loved every minute of our trip in the bazaars. We had been bewitched by the noise, bustle, crowds and the clamour and spellbound by the unbelievable variety of goods for sale.

What is more, we had penetrated and explored areas of the bazaar where few seemed to venture...but the bats.

Up the Khyber Pass

We left Peshawar behind and drove in convoy westwards past dried-up river beds and the refugee camps.

The sandy coloured hills shimmered in the heat haze across the plains. At the check point we were stopped by dark hawkeyed tribesmen carrying guns and wearing bandoliers. They checked everybody that went through. There was a queue of cars, the regular merchants that traded up the pass, and the buses that service the villages. The railway line ran along beside the road that still carries a weekly train up the pass from Peshawar to Landi Kotal.

We were an official party escorted by police, so we were waved quickly through, but not until we had been subjected to intensely curious stares through the windows.

Between the check point and the pass was a wide open plain bereft of habitation except for Jamrud Fort. Tribesmen wandered down the road all carrying guns. There was no mistaking the opening to the pass. On a prominent hilltop stood a stone picket. Those soldiers of old had a perfect position to observe movements coming through the pass, be they friend or foe.

Today the soldiers have a different target. Pakistan has become one of the major producers of opium and heroin. The tribespeople have discovered that they can grow a vast wealth-producing commodity. The local administrators have tried to stop it by punishments and fines for those caught peddling and producing drugs. As always they take no notice. They are secure in the knowledge that no one will venture into their territory without fearing for their lives. Predictably they refuse to give up a cheap and easy means of income since the opium poppy grows in profusion up in the mountains.

Since December 1982 the authorities had not been able to guarantee safe passage up the pass. The numbers of those to whom permission is granted was drastically reduced. We were fortunate in being allowed up there before the regulations were brought in.

We passed the sandy coloured villages surrounded by their high walls made of mud. Watch towers were built at the corners with slits for rifles. Their privacy was guarded as jealously as their territory. We could see the old

Ali Masjid Fort, Khyber Pass

railway threading its way through the countless tunnels up the length of the pass. Like an overloaded caterpillar it crawled in and out of the rabbit holes carved out of the mountain. The locals are allowed to use the railway free of charge as a concession agreed by the British when the tribes people allowed them to build the railway through their territory. A little bribery seems to have gone a long way!

The mountains with their jagged peaks towered over us as we drove the 35 miles through the Pass; every ridge, hill and vantage point was topped with a lookout. Nothing could pass by without being seen. At one point the Shagai Fort dominated the Pass. It was a huge, walled, impregnable fortress built by the British in 1920. On the side of the hill it cast a sinister brooding eye on all below. We had not been given permission to visit the Fort. From the road we could see the training area, games pitches, and soldiers doing weapon training.

From the top of the hair pin bends we could see spectacular views back down the Pass to Peshawar. It was possible to see the old road, narrow and little used nowadays by the heavy traffic. I longed for somebody to tell us the tales of the skirmishes and battles of old, and to reconstruct the scenes of history that surrounded us. Being swept along in a cavalcade we had neither the time nor the opportunity to stop and be told of the past.

It was after the First Afghan War in 1842 that the British made a paved road through the pass. They built the pickets and forts along its length to prevent a possible invasion of the sub continent by the Russians. The Pathans fiercely resisted anybody encroaching on their territory as they wanted to continue raiding the camel caravans and to gather the safe conduct money unmolested. The British had to pay the Pathans to keep the peace, allowing them to run their own affairs.

There were countless skirmishes against the British, and tribe fought against tribe. The British exacted their revenge by razing whole villages to the ground. It was a turbulent area where each side had a healthy respect for the other.

We stopped at the smuggler's town of Landi Kotal. Down in the bazaars were the alleyways, dingy doorways and open drains and vegetable stalls swarming with flies. Kebabs were being cooked on open fires and old men were mending and soling shoes with old car tyres. Here can be bought silks, cameras, electrical goods and no doubt opium and heroin, and illegal goods of all sorts. One of our number disappeared down one of the alleyways later to return with three rifles slung over his shoulder!

We stopped once more on a rocky hilltop with a police picket beside the Pass. It has a wonderful view down the valley towards Torkam in the distance. Below us a trail of pack donkeys wound their way across a stony ridge, escorted by women wearing brightly coloured clothes. They must have been Afghans. Just below us two old men sat perched on a boulder puffing contentedly on their hookahs while they gazed down the valley. Above us on a wide plateau, almost invisible since it was fashioned from the earth around it, was a small village. It looked deserted, but who knew who might be watching from up there? There was a constant movement of buses and lorries labouring up and down the winding pass.

Further along beside the roadside were large boulders that had been carved and painted with Regimental crests, a proud memorial to those who had fallen in battle up the pass. We took a side road and followed smart white painted stones that led up to the camp of the Khyber Rifles Regiment.

We were met by extremely well turned out military police who saluted and signalled us to the Officers' Mess. We were made very welcome by the officers and we caught our first sight of the soldiers of this prestigious regiment wearing their distinctive uniform of grey shalwar chemise with their red sashes and puggarees.

Inside the Mess we relaxed in the cool anteroom, the men separated from the women. Here we could see the wonderful mementoes, plaques and portraits presented by visitors or those that had served there. I wandered off to look at the silver, paintings, gifts and photographs of the old campaigners. Here at last were the old bewhiskered soldiers, very upright in their chairs staring fixedly at the camera. Beside them were their colleagues wearing turbans and puggarees and a grim self conscious expression. What a lot of English names and faces! I wondered where their descendants were today? Perhaps their families have identical pictures in their photograph albums.

From the Khyber Rifles Mess it was but a short drive to the border town of Torkham. At the border there was a customs check point, an immigration office and a tourist rest house. There was also a prominent notice forbidding the photography of tribal women. There seemed to be few formalities at the border as the carts and traps wandered through. As we arrived, the border was closed so a small crowd had gathered on either side. The road that led on into Afghanistan was shady and tree lined. A few miles on the scenery opened out to a vista of undulating hills. After the dusty and arid mountains of the pass it was a fertile land of trees and shrubs.

Beside the barrier there was a flight of steps to a view point. Across the border the Afghan flag fluttered. It was hard to believe, looking at this peaceful scene that there was a war going on, and the Russians were only fifteen miles away.

Peasants the world over are concerned with little but their meagre livelihood and working their land. Who is in power has little relevance to them unless the going gets tough. For the Afghans the going was very tough. After the Russian invasion of their country their scarce and valuable food was being utilised by the Soviet troops. It was increasingly difficult to scratch a living from the land that had been bombed and mined. Famine was not far away. In desperation families had fled to Iran and Pakistan. The young and eligible had stayed to fight with a ferocious determination to rid their country of the hated Russian bear.

The Russians underestimated these fierce Afghan people who had been born in the hills and possessed the cunning of their forefathers. It has been said that to conquer the Afghan resistance it was necessary to throw forces numbering ten to one against them.

The quiet country road a few yards from where we stood had offered a road to freedom. Would it again, as it had for centuries, become a gateway for an invader?

We visit the Afghan Refugees

Since the invasion of Afghanistan by the Soviet Union in 1979 thousands of refugees had poured over the borders of Pakistan hoping to find help and a home. They had made their way over the passes and the mountains of Baluchistan. The people of Afghanistan speak Pushto and many local dialects so on arrival they try to locate their own tribe within the camps set up for them.

The numbers had soared to three million and their presence had become a huge burden for Pakistan, itself a far from wealthy country. Help had to come from elsewhere. Much of it was provided by the United Nations High Commission for Refugees, United Nations Aid agencies, the World Food Programme and anyone else who could help. The cost of providing for these people was about 1.5 million US dollars a day. Pakistan was paying 43% of the cost, the rest had to come from foreign aid. There is a fear that the supply of aid may dry up. It was five years since it had begun and what had started as an emergency problem seemed to be turning into a permanent commitment. The goodwill of the donor nations was being sorely stretched.

When the refugees arrived they had to register in the North West Frontier Province and in Baluchistan. Issued with Rs120 or £6 they were also given shelter, tents, bedding, blankets and a quilt. They were also issued with one pair of shoes a year, some used clothing, and lengths of cotton. There was a ration of 8 metres for men, 13 metres for the women and 4 metres for the children. They were given cooking utensils, a cooking stove, and kerosene. A generous donation by anyone's standards.

In Peshawar there was a hospital run solely for the use of the freedom fighters from Afghanistan, by the International Red Cross. Dedicated doctors and nurses worked around the clock treating and operating on patients with war injuries. Many would have had to travel for two or three weeks in jeep, truck or van from the furthest regions of Afghanistan to get there. In the Afghan camps there were health units provided with specialist doctors and nurses. There were X ray units and clinics for artificial limbs. There were 130 dispensaries, 71 mobile medical units, and for the children there were 70 primary schools. There were also 23 centres that taught carpet weaving, farming, irrigation, forestry and veterinary training. I wondered how much was provided for them at home?

The refugees were not encouraged to own their own businesses, since that would have given them a permanent footing in the country, a prospect that the Government of Pakistan was not anxious to encourage. Since the tents became very hot in the summer the refugees built mud houses to provide some shelter from the blazing heat, and to provide them with some added privacy.

By the roadside we were interested to see how they constructed their walls. Five men were building a wall 15ft high. One man poured water on a mud patch. A second mixed up a mud pat, a third heaved it up to a fourth man on a ladder, who then threw it up to the wall builder on the top. He caught it, slapped it, patted and then smoothed it down. When it was finished the wall was about 14 inches thick. When baked in the sun it became as hard as concrete. An admirable protection against the sun and the rain.

Behind these walls a huge community lived. Afghan women were more fiercely protected and were also more shy and retiring than their Pakistani counterparts. Within the high walled mud compound they were assured of privacy and protection from prying eyes. We saw Afghan women in their colourful smocks and baggy trousers. They wore dresses with smocked bodices that fell in thick gathered folds to below their knees. Underneath they wore full baggy trousers that were caught into embroidered cuffs at the ankles. They covered their dresses at the cuffs and hems with delicate stitching which made their clothes a work of art. They often wore heavy bangles and neck chains, and sometimes they had a thin metal edging to their veils.

We watched them while they washed their big metal pots, pitchers and plates in the stream that ran beside the road. They scoured them with mud and grass, rinsed them in the stream and then they stacked them one on top of the other on their heads to carry them back to the camp. Menfolk kept a wary protective eye over their women, ready to lift a gun at the slightest provocation.

Children with tangled hair and grimy clothes played under the trees swinging on branches or old tyres, or tumbling about in the dirt. Some of the older girls were watching their mothers, or helping to fetch and carry water.

The boys were with their fathers making door frames, mending bikes or building mud walls.

We passed some boys who were playing with their stumpy little catapults. They were firing pebbles at a lamp post 50 metres away with deadly accuracy. It was a powerful little weapon. Colin soon drew an amused crowd as he tried his hand with the catapult. The crowd wanted to know from where we had come, and from which country.

As we went into the camp we were followed down the mudwalled alleyways by a crowd of curious children. Veiled women half-hidden, peeped out from behind walls and doorways to see where we were going. We had been given permission to go inside one of their homes. We went to a family home secluded behind the back of the compound. Made completely of mud, it had no windows. A low doorway led to a room about 12ft by 8ft. It was big enough to sleep eight people stretched out on the floor. There was no furniture, but at one end there were shelves to stack bedding, personal bundles and cooking pots. In the middle of the room was a cleverly made fireplace; fashioned in mud it would be stoked with sticks. It had a chimney leading up vertically to the roof. It was cool and dark inside.

An old lady greeted us with a large grin. She was obviously accustomed to guests and she was neither shy nor retiring. She wore a green and purple embroidered bodice with purple baggy trousers. Her dupatta and sleeves were edged with heavy metal dangles, and she wore a matching heavy necklace and bracelets. Cheerful and relaxed, she shook our hands and made us very welcome. As we sat down on the floor two girls, heavily veiled, who were in the hut with her, turned to the walls and covered their heads. They refused to let us see their faces. Not for the first time I admired the way that women drop with practised ease to sit cross-legged on the floor.

Through an interpreter the old lady told us a little about her family. They had come to Pakistan two years previously and had been in the camp all that time. She had seven sons all of whom were fighting with the Mudjahadeen over the border. The two girls with her were married to her sons. They had no idea when they would return home. They came home for brief intervals and then returned to the fighting. She had no idea where they were. She seemed to accept stoically the situation and the absence of her sons. Of her husband there was neither sign nor mention.

The old lady offered us green tea and a small broken biscuit which we shared cross-legged on the floor. She could not do enough for us and apologised for the humble fare. We wished very much we could have given her something in return and regretted coming empty handed. We were very humbled by her widow's mite.

We had the opportunity to see the elders of the tribe at a welcoming ceremony under some shamianas set up on the stony hillside. These fierce uncompromising warriors from over the border sat grouped on the ground facing us. We were fascinated to see at close quarters this proud warlike race against whom few have prevailed. They clutched the guns no Afghan would be seen without. These robed figures with their sharp eyes, black beards and lean suntanned faces under their turbans left us in no doubt that they were as ready as coiled springs to leap into battle to defend their home land. There was a formal welcome from one of the elders who proclaimed their gratitude for the group's interest and concern for their predicament. Our spokesman in reply pledged continued support and encouragement for their cause. It was greeted with enthusiastic leaps in the air and shouts of "Huzzah". However they needed more than words of sympathy and compassion from us Westerners.

Market stalls of all kinds have been set up for the refugees on the roadside. Since the Afghans have been dissuaded from owning their own premises, many of the carpet and silver merchants sought their fortunes by taking to the road with their wares. They chanced their luck on the highways and in the bazaars. There were some who were not Afghans, or refugees, who were cashing in on the sympathy of an unsuspecting public by posing as such.

It is felt by some and resented by others that the Afghan refugees were in many cases a great deal better off than their Pakistani counterparts and neighbours. That is as may be, but the fact remained that their future was uncertain. They had been dispossessed of their home land. From what we had seen at the refugee camp we were under no illusion that they intended to return home at the first opportunity.

Dawn in the mountains

Grey with sleep the mountains and valley await
The warm touch of the sun.
A breathless peace casts a spell.
Motionless, expectant,
The watching trees, sentinels of the night
Wait for the dawnrise of the day.
The birds are hushed
The patient flowers, their faces washed with dew
Watch from their leafy beds.
Yonder over distant peaks
A crescendo of light
Announces that the sun is at hand.
There....
The lord of the mountains
King of the peaks
Receives his golden crown,
An accolade of age.
Then, messengers of sunlight
Running ever downwards,
Crack and crevice,
All are bestowed with the golden dust.
The valley wakes.

Flight to Skardu

From Afghanistan in the west to Nepal in the east gigantic mountain ridges of jagged white teeth form a barrier between the Soviet Union in the north west and China in the north east. Along the Afghan border the Hindu Kush edges round to join the Karakorams. Here three giants rear their lofty heads, K2 close to the Chinese border is 28,250 ft, Nanga Parbat 26,660 ft and Rakaposhi 25,550ft. Further east in the Himalayas, the king of them all reigns supreme; Mt Everest 29,002 ft. In troughs and ridges they lie in frozen stillness as far as the eye can see in a deserted white wilderness.

Only the stout-hearted come to test their endurance on the peaks. The qualifications, restrictions, and the mountaineering fees demanded have deterred many. The risks and dangers for those given permission to take on the highest mountains in the world, are high. When measured against these geological giants man is very small indeed.

These mighty snows are the bountiful providers of life-giving water without which Pakistan would revert to desert. Beneath these icy wastes trickles the water of life that seeps down the mountain side joining the streams and waterfalls that tumble into the rivers in the valley below. From all along the mountain ranges the Rivers Kunar, Kabul, Swat and Indus bring their cool fresh water to join the Jhelum, the Chinab, Ravi and Sutlej rivers which carry it down to the parched plains.

It is from these plains that people scurry to the valleys at the weekend or on holiday. Running like tributaries from the Great Trunk Road from Lahore to Peshawar, the roads and tracks lead off up northwards beside the rivers into the valleys of Chitral, Swat, Gilgit and Hunza. It is here that they can photograph the distant peaks, trek up the passes and rugged glaciers, fish in the rivers, explore the valleys or ancient sites. Everywhere the scenery was spell binding. Each valley had its own character and charm as they changed their cloak of colour with the seasons. Only the mountains never changed. We wanted to see them for ourselves.

Every day if the conditions were right, a little Fokker Friendship aircraft leaves Islamabad airport at dawn when the air is still and calm. It flies in supplies and tourists to Skardu, an isolated town sixty miles south of K2 and the Chinese border. Many tourists remain there for a few days, others, like us, go for the ride, returning on the same day. Confirming our seats the evening before, we set off for Rawalpindi at 4.00 am long before anyone was about.

It was peaceful and quiet on the deserted roads in the early dawn. The buses and lorries had been laid to rest. Peace reigned and the daily clamour was abated. It was a lovely time of the day. One or two shrouded figures like Lazarus rose up and were shuffling off to work. Goats were roaming the streets and picking over the refuse. One or two shops were coming to life and stiffened arms were being stretched after clutching blankets all night.

At the airport there was a seething mob of people who had come to meet the incoming flights. We had to push our way through the crowds to reach the Northern Areas Office. Here a mass of bodies were pushing and shoving around the only counter. Somebody was having trouble with their ticket. Why is it that whenever we want to fly anywhere there is always someone having trouble with their tickets ahead of us in the queue? The crowd, enjoying every minute, were leaning over the counter watching the proceedings, giving advice and sympathy. There were piles of blankets and bundles, and battered old suitcases tied up with what looked like forty yards of brightly coloured clothes line, aged belts and string.

Into this cotton clamour we plunged to have our tickets checked. All eyes swung in our direction. Being the only Europeans we became the new diversion. Feeling confident that all was in order we were dismayed to find that we had not been booked on the flight at all. The grins and mutters intensified around us. The fact that we had been booked on the flight by the Asian Study Group meant nothing.

Then others in the group began to arrive. They were not on the list either. We were beginning to feel not a little silly and very angry.

We retreated for consultation.

"We must see the management."

A deputation was sent to complain. Squaring their shoulders and giving an indignant sniff the men went off. They got....nowhere. At this point a smartly dressed woman came in.

"Is this the flight to Skardu?" she yelled over the hullabaloo, waving her tickets over her head. She vanished.

She was probably flattened by a bed roll.

There was nothing for it but to go to the PIA office when it opened and see if we could get on the 11am flight.

Two sleepy officers lolling in their chairs struggled upright as we walked in, gazing at us with bleary eyed disinterest.

Colin repeated our question, "Is this the flight for Skardu?"

"No," they replied. "The flight to Skardu was full, at 11am. Try another day."

"What name was it?" one of them asked. "A Brigadier?"

There was an immediate thaw in the temperature.

Colin, not to be mollified, told them what a poor show it was. He could understand difficulties with the weather as he was a pilot himself..

"You, a pilot?" they asked, beginning to suspect as much.

When Colin admitted that he was, the temperature rose even more

"But of course you will be on the flight today...ek minute..."

Suddenly the phones were humming to Skardu and confident smiles were sent in our direction. Within minutes we were presented with our tickets with the compliments of PIA! I half expected them to invite Colin to fly the aeroplane! Goodness knows who the poor souls were who had been put off the flight.

Clutching our tickets we returned to the Airport thinking our problems were over. We did not have a very encouraging start.

"What is that?" asked a policeman, confronting Colin.

Colin looked around to see if there was an offending piece of baggage.

"No, that," he said pointing to me.

Colin was furious. "That is my wife, now will you please get out of my way."

Back inside the customs checked our belongings. In case we were marooned up in Skardu by weather I had packed my sponge bag. The officer pulled it out and proceeded to go through everything with a tooth comb, holding up my most personal items for everybody else to see. When he had quite finished I was dismissed and waved into a side room for the Begums.

Empty of chairs and tables it was like a cattle pen with concrete walls. Slumped in a corner on the floor was a woman with her child. Beaten and defeated into submission she had accepted her lot and had no voice of protest.

But I had! I was furious when I heard Colin had been invited to sit in luxury in the VIP lounge! Wondering where I had got to he was horrified to find me shut away in this cell. He told me to come with him. Such treatment was intolerable. It was obvious to get any consideration one had to be assertive, aggressive and demanding. Everything worked if you had chits, passes, authorities and special permission. In Pakistan the magic wand was a military rank, preferably a senior one. Wives of any rank seemed to count not at all.

It was not over yet. The flight was called. They wished to see tickets and baggage checks. It appeared that I did not have one. They wanted to search my baggage again, so the whole beastly business was repeated. Frisked, scanned and scrutinised they considered finally that I was fit to fly... but no..!

At the steps of the plane we were stopped again. What was the trouble now? Colin had a boarding card but I didn't have one!

"Come with me..come." I was ordered by the airport police.

That did it. The early start, their offensive treatment, their impertinent attitude towards me that had been simmering for some time blew up. The Memsahib let fly an earful of pretty unprintable language. I had had enough... I was heartily sick of being pushed about... Consternation...Begums do not normally answer back, or refuse to obey. What to do? The airport police looked at each other. There were whispers and mutters. There were two sides of opinion. There was the "Pro Mem" group who thought I should get away with it and "Anti Mem" group who thought a stand should be made...women in their place etc....impasse. In the end it was the pilot who decided it. He was beckoning out of the cockpit window indicating in no uncertain way to get on with it. He wanted to be off. Reluctantly the officer took out his pencil, chewed the end, looked at me speculatively, and scribbled the Urdu equivalent of OK on the ticket and waved us aboard.

It was worth all the humiliations once we were airborne. The flight was pure magic. The skies were calm and cloudless as we soared up and over Islamabad and turned northwards over the Margalla Hills. We climbed up over the brown foothills with the terracing on their slopes and within minutes we could see ahead the peaks with their sprinkle of snowy icing sugar. Far into the distance they unfolded before us. Soon we were surrounded by glorious snow scapes with swooping valleys of untrodden snow, gullies, crevasses and jagged ridges. Ice pinnacles frozen solid overlaid rocky escarpments frosted like a refrigerator. The brilliant sun lit up the summits into dazzling whiteness whilst casting blue shadows into the valley. We could see K2 head and shoulders above its neighbours in the distance clearly visible against the blue sky. We flew close beside Nanga Parbat, our shadow running beside us on its flank.

The crew, obliging and helpful, allowed us into the cockpit to get a better view. I squeezed in behind the pilot wedged tightly amongst the knobs and switches. I took the golden opportunity to film the panorama below.

Ahead we could see Skardu. It lay on a plateau deep in the mountains. Brown and barren it looked, bare of vegetation. As we circled down towards it, the mountains closed in on all sides. On the approach the pilot forgot to tell me to return to my seat and being of no mind to remind him I remained where I was. I was thrilled to have the opportunity to film an aircraft landing... from the cockpit window.

Once on the ground I was predictably refused to film the airport, although there was nothing there except a runway. The airport buildings were still under construction. There were no facilities at all where we could get a drink or to attend to the call of nature. I did manage to get my own back on the police in a small way. I persuaded a vain uniformed policeman standing by to have his photograph taken. Could he move just a little bit?... there...and bit more? Thank you! He had no idea that he had been nicely placed in front of the aeroplane!

We were struck by the slant eyes of the workmen. We guessed that they were of Chinese or Tibetan extraction. We had no chance to see any other inhabitants, since the town of Skardu was a few miles away. There was a hotel there called the Shangrila which was a haven for guests who wished to get away from it all, though perhaps for longer than intended... if the planes cannot fly.. or the roads are blocked with snow.

Our stay was brief, long enough only to refuel the plane. In no time we were circling up and over the plateau. Down below we could see the fingers of the muddy river resembling brown paint spilt on the floor of the valley. On top of the encircling mountains a thin wreath of cloud was beginning to form. We had got out just in time.

We had had a breathtaking flight. The weather had been perfect and the views unbelievable. As we flew back we gazed below and gave respectful thought to those who by means of ropes, crampons, and ice axes climbed crawled and clambered with resolution, determination and daring to the tops of those icy summits, to see the view that we had seen... without any effort at all... Well, almost!

The Swat Valley

Over the enturies the Swat valley has seen a succession of settlers who saw fit to live, fight or leave remains there. Stone Age people lived there. Aryans from Central Asia, Alexander the Great invaded the Swat valley on their way to the Indus. The Buddhists came in the second century and stayed there for 700 years. Hindu kings built forts there. The Moghuls came and saw but did not conquer. Even Winston Churchill came there. We hoped to find and explore his picket.

In the 19th century one man, the Akund of Swat, a good and holy man united the whole valley people. His descendants became the Walis or rulers of Swat in India. In 1926 Swat became a separate state and in 1969 it became a district of Pakistan.

We took the road to Mardan where there was a major military base. It is the HQ of the elite Corps of Guides. The Guides had been the first British soldiers to wear khaki. The bright red and blue uniforms of the British soldiers had been too easy a target for the Pathan snipers. In the centre of Mardan was an imposing memorial arch to the Guides who died in Kabul at the storming of the Residency in Afghanistan. There is an account of the action in M M Kaye's book *The Far Pavilions*. The plaque on the arch reads:- "The annals of no Army and no regiment can show a brighter record of devoted bravery than has been achieved by this small band of Guides. By their deeds they have conferred undying honour not only on the Regiment to which they belong, but to the whole British Army."

Several miles ahead we could see the bare bleak hills of the Malakand Pass of Nicholson fame. Dry barren and treeless it would have provided little cover for fugitives. It presents a formidable barrier to the Swat valley. At the top of the pass was the Malakand Fort where the Sikhs under British command held off 10,000 tribal warriors during the Pathan uprising in 1897.

A road winds its way up the pass around hairpin bends, carved like a ledge it was quite a feat of engineering. Sheep, goats, donkeys and families on the move plodded slowly up the pass undeterred by the cars, buses and lorries that steamed and hissed their way past. From the top of the pass there was a spectacular view back down the valley, green with crops and grass while the plains faded away into the distance and the heat haze.

There was an encampment of Afghans beside the road, the women recognisable by their colourful clothes, embroidered bodices and full flowing skirts. We wondered if they would run away when we stopped to watch them.

Afghan women, Malakand Pass

Surprisingly they were as interested in us as we in them and they even allowed me to take photographs. They were considerably less retiring than their sisters in the camps.

On the other side of the pass the scenery changed to a lush patchwork of fields, foliage and flowers. Fishermen were casting their nets into the river, and farmers were busy in the fields. Women were washing their clothes in the streams, carrying water on their heads or loads of wattle for fencing. Everywhere long-stemmed buttercups and poppies waved in the breeze. Here was a beautiful fertile valley beside the broad reaches of the River Swat.

As we approached Chakdara, across the river we could see Churchill's Picket perched on a hill top. It was in that eagle's eyrie that he had stayed for four months in 1897 while he reported to *The London Daily Telegraph* the Pathan uprising. We crossed over the river, parked the Land Rover by Chakdara Fort, and climbed the track up to the picket. We clambered up the very steep steps to the entrance and crawled in through a hatch-like window. The room inside was about 20ft by 30ft with a high ceiling. It was bare but for an old fireplace. There was a ladder leading up to a flat roof. There was an unbelievable view from the rooftop in all directions up and down the valleys. What a wonderful lookout. It provided a splendid hideaway and bolt hole.

Inside it wasn't too difficult to imagine Winston Churchill sitting there at a table, perhaps with a fire in the hearth, a charpoy, lantern, cooking pots in the corner and washing facilities of the simplest kind. The reports that he wrote were vivid and descriptive.

"There was a ragged volley from the rocks, shouts and exclamations, a scream. One man was shot through the breast and was pouring with blood, another lay kicking and twisting. The British Officer was spinning around just behind me, his face a mass of blood, his right eye cut out. Yes it certainly was an adventure."

That I would have thought was an understatement!

The moment we pulled in for petrol we became the objects of local interest. At least twenty men having nothing whatever to do ambled over to the Land Rover to have a good look inside. Since their interest might prevail sufficiently to tempt them into putting their hand through the windows, cameras were hurriedly hidden out of sight. Inquisitive faces peered in the window. No words were spoken as I was being minutely scrutinised from head to toe from twelve inches away. Increasingly uncomfortable under their curious stares, I was delighted when we were on the move again. The teeming throngs of men in the streets parted like a tide around a rock as we tried to get through the town.

Saidu Sharif was the home of the Prince and Princess of Swat. A circular drive led to a delightful bungalow set about by a spacious verandah and a beautiful peaceful garden.

Miangul Aurenzeb is the present ruler of Swat. His father, now an old man, is still revered greatly by the valley people. The heritage of good and wise administration had fallen to his son Miangul who now represents Swat in the Madjlis or Parliament in Islamabad. He spends his time between duties in the city and in the valley where he holds open court for people at any time of the day. On his verandah he listens to the problems and disputes that come up and he gives advice and assistance when he can. He makes himself available to his people at all times. Being the informal and friendly man he is, it was not surprising that the humble people found him so approachable.

Naseem, his charming wife, was the daughter of the late Field Marshal Ayub Khan, who was the first military President of Pakistan. As his daughter she accompanied him on his travels meeting the crowned heads of Europe, also the Prime Ministers and Presidents of countries world wide. A regal and serene lady, she exuded calm and dignity. It was with these two delightful people we were honoured to stay.

We sat outside on the lawns to have tea, waited on by servants smartly dressed in uniforms and puggarees. It was a typical English tea served from a silver tea pot on a silver tray. As dusk came down across the valley the distant hills were tinged with pink in the sunset. Later at dinner we listened spellbound to their experiences and travels of the past and we were shown their fascinating collection of photographs. Being the thoughtful hosts they were they sought to make us feel at home by playing music from the Royal Tournament at Earls Court! Also by serving us dinner of English food. This gracious couple could not have made us more welcome.

The next day we followed the river north. The valley closed in and the hills narrowed around us. We stopped at the town of Khwazakhela to look at curios by the roadside. There was an intriguing collection of old carved wooden boards, unidentifiable wooden platters, implements, tools, stools and huge wooden ladles. There were gate posts, wooden clogs, tribal charms, pewter dangles, thimbles, coins and stones, both rough and the polished variety. Poking about in the trays and boxes I hoped to find some local mineral to add to my collection. There was an emerald mine up the Swat valley in which they have found stones of good quality. In a dark corner covered in dust I found what I was looking for. Elsewhere there were smocks, dresses, and the caps that were worn by all the men in the Northern areas. Colin tried a cap on and decided it was for him. I bought a beautiful woven shawl and a typical smocked dress.

The river that had wandered peacefully down the lower regions was in a different mood up there. Mighty rushing torrents of turquoise water hurtled downstream, bubbling and swirling around grey boulders sculpted into weird shapes. The road unveiled at each corner ever more glorious views. The white tops of the mountains peeped at us from around the shoulders of the lower inclines. The Land Rover had to paddle through the glacier tails melting across the road. We passed through Madyan and Bahrain stopping to buy fruit and honey.

On the mountains on each side the farmers had levelled the almost vertical slopes for growing wheat and maize. Perched up among the stone walls, mud-roofed houses nestled into the slopes. Water mills ground the grain between huge mill stones, taking advantage of every tributary that flowed down to the Swat.

Family on the move; Swat Valley

The villagers were friendly as we passed by and here the women were less shy. Although there was work to be done in the fields they could not resist a speculative interest in visitors that passed by. We passed a solidly built school set in among the pine trees. School had just ended. The boys were dressed in grey cotton shalwar chemise and blue berets with a red diamond on the front. They all carried school slates, which came in handy to clout each other as they played in the dust! We saw no little girls. Their life was one of work in hearth and home. Further up the valley the road ran out from under the pine trees and ahead on a plateau with a gorgeous view across the valley to Mt Falaksir (20,528ft) were the rest houses of Kalam and the Falaksir Hotel.

We stopped here for lunch, the only guests in the dingy dining room with its grubby table cloths, flyblown windows and greasy floors. Primitive in the extreme, with limited lighting, no hot water, guests needed to be aware of what to expect, and to bring their own soap, basin plugs, candles and clean sheets. With rest houses in this state it was little wonder that NW Pakistan did not feature in the world's tourist brochures. The breathtaking mountains would be seen by only the most hardy and least complaining of trekkers.

Beyond Kalam the road became a gravel track that ran up into the pine trees. The snow covered mountains towered above and the waterfalls splashed into the river far down below. We came to a clearing of open ground and there in a magical position was the Deodar Rest house. Sleeping six, it was booked privately by individuals for much of the year. We were lucky it was deserted. We sat on the steps and listened to the breathless hush, the call of the birds in the forest, and drank in the warm scented smell of the pine trees. We wandered into the woods and picked up the sweet smelling chips of wood left by a woodcutter, and hand fulls of little rose shaped cones. It must be one of the most beautiful and peaceful spots in Pakistan. We resolved that one day we would return, and soak in the atmosphere of that most heavenly place.

Further up the valley isolated communities lived in their mud-roofed homes. Where they could, they tilled, ploughed and planted. They were able to grow melons and potatoes and they kept bees. There was a well known brand of Swat honey. Their flat-roofed houses were constructed of a framework of timber. The spaces between were tightly plugged with rocks and stones similar to dry stone walling in England. They would have to be substantial structures since for much of the winter they were under snow. They funnelled the water from the mountain streams into their homes by means of long shallow troughs made of timber. They had a permanent cold water system on hand. The only drawback was they could never turn the tap off! Those at subsistence level lived in pathetically poor conditions in the upper reaches of the valley. Ragged little children crawled out from homes that were little more than twigs propped up against a tree.

Wayfarers with laden donkeys and mules wended their way slowly down the track, picking their way over the pebbles and rough ground. One man had a large animal skin that he had cured over his shoulder. They paid no heed to us and hardly gave us a glance as they passed by. One old man stumbled along carrying a huge load of green branches and twigs. As he passed by we offered him a cold drink and a biscuit. We noticed that instead of shoes on his feet he had a covering of sacking and skins. Unwilling to waste time with strangers he paused long enough to accept our drink, take a handful of biscuits and then he stumbled off down the track.

In a clearing men were levering pine logs three feet in diameter onto a lorry. The road was becoming increasingly difficult as we bounced over rough tracks and lurched over narrow bridges made of pine logs. It was obvious that we were reaching the head of the valley. Finally the track gave out. There ahead was Lake Mohadand. It was a scene straight out of the Canadian Rockies. The valley had widened out into a bowl surrounding a mirror flat lake. A small spit of land edged it with some pine trees, some logs lay submerged. It was breathlessly still. It would not have surprised us to see beavers at work. We knew that there were bears in the mountains.

From the direction of the Chinese border a few miles to the north two figures came into sight. As they came nearer we saw that it was an old man and his son bent over with the weight of two huge brass urns. How far they had walked we had no means of knowing. Since there was no habitation this far up the valley we guessed that they had come over the mountains by the Kachikani Pass from either Gilgit or Chitral. They could have walked anything from 20 to 100 miles over wild trekking country. Slowly they disappeared down the track and we were alone.

The stillness and the majesty of the mountains of Swat had the effect of silencing mere man. We were hushed by their tranquil immobility and over awed by their timelessness. Thrown up there by the mighty forces of nature millions of years ago, so they will remain for millions of years to come.

The clouds came down as softly as thistle down over the mountains, forming mufflers around their icy necks. The mountains, having given a magnificent display and silenced their audience, were now preparing to leave the stage.

Rockslip

At midnight it became clear that something had stirred the gods of the mountains. It began with distant flickers of lightning and muffled rumbles of thunder. Suddenly the battle grew nearer and a resounding crash announced that the gods had taken up positions on opposing mountain tops in the Kaghan valley. Electric sparks rent the air and flickers of light reflected their parrying swords. Ominous rumbles echoed off the mountain. There were cracks like machine gun fire, and hail the size of mothballs rattled and bounced onto our tin roof.

Water fell out of the sky like a running bath tap, smacked down on the roof, sprayed out horizontally into the windows. As if to clinch the matter the god on our side planted his thousand pound gun right outside our room and with an earsplitting crack fired a million volts across the valley. I leapt out of my skin and straight into Colin's bed. This coup de grace seemed to have the desired effect of taming the opposition who, sensing defeat, gathered his cloak of darkness around him and backed off over the mountain spitting sparks of anger and rumbling revenge. We felt certain that some of the little houses would have been washed away in the night and would be lying in heaps at the bottom of the mountain. We were relieved to see that they were still firmly fixed to the mountain!

We began the long drive home. The river was an angry torrent. The turquoise bubbles yesterday had changed to a swirling muddy tide that gushed full speed downstream, carrying with it pebbles and branches that were being hurtled into it from the swollen mountain streams. A low mist shrouded the mountains, and valley.

Skirting around pebbles and small rocks that had washed onto the road in the storm, we turned a corner and found to our dismay that our way was blocked by a massive rock slip, 200 tons of rock had literally slipped down the mountain during the night and landed on the road. Impasse. We stood about in the drenching rain wondering what to do. A queue of cars built up behind us, their owners defeated and glum.

Two of our party decided to investigate the possibility of picking up some form of transport from the other side. The news was good, a bus was waiting on the far side and ready to go.

Rockslip, Kaghan Valley

We had a family discussion to decide who should go on ahead in the bus. There were eight of us, including our grandson Duncan, aged 14 months. There were family flight schedules to keep. There seemed no choice. We would all have to go on ahead, reluctantly leaving Colin and Razak to bring back the Land Rover and the Staff car. We clambered over the rockslip and made our way to the bus with the few possessions that we could carry. In conditions that could hardly be worse with mud and water on the slippery roads and mile upon mile of narrow ledges and corners to negotiate I was distinctly apprehensive. I was even more so when I saw how many other people were climbing on as well.

We squeezed ourselves along the bench at the back that had just enough head and foot room. Old men and young men with turbans and beards carrying sacks and bundles pushed their way in and in no time we were surrounded by rags and wrinkles, hens and hookahs. Bundles had many uses. They could be used as bedrolls, grips or kit bags. They could contain anything from logs to chickens.

Headgear of all sorts was worn. Cloths were wound round, twisted up and folded over and down over flashing eyes, dark skin and black hair. More and more grubby hands grabbed the rail and swung into the bus with muddy feet and ill fitting chapplis. They swarmed, pushed and edged into every crack and cranny and finally found the only place left, a square inch by the door. If one of us had wanted to change our minds because of claustrophobia or suffocation there was no way we could have extricated ourselves from there, we were hermetically sealed in.

With a trumpeting sound the bus announced that its charge down the hill was about to begin. Hanging onto Duncan, our grandson, and the pillow, we thankfully had thought to bring, we lurched off down the road. Our cameras and overnight bags were submerged under skinny legs and ankles. At every corner the bus gave a hoot which made Duncan yell as he bounced like a ping pong ball on his pillow.

Cushioned by steaming humanity we swayed and heaved shoulder to shoulder. The bus eased itself over ruts and hummocks in the road like an old lady who had difficulty shifting her undercarriage. Mudslips and minor rockslips retreated behind us as we crawled along the ledges.

We had plenty of time to study our companions. The man just in front of us was wearing a white cap. He had a large mouth with large teeth inside it. Much of what he had to say must have been amusing since the audience sitting close by went off into raucous laughter at fairly regular intervals. There was a teacher of English but he was unwilling to talk to us.

At one stop an old man tried to get in. He managed to get as far as the bottom step where he squeezed enough space to settle down and seemed quite impervious to the milling throngs that fell in or out around him. He even managed to go to sleep. Further down the road he was eventually rolled out of the door still sound asleep, trodden on by the heaving hordes.

The smell of soggy cotton, grubby clothes and unwashed bodies became overpowering. We all steamed slowly and the windows misted up. From time to time we turned thankfully to our windows for a breath of air.

People got on and off all down the valley. There was much clambering up the back ladder to the roof. At one stop we counted 25 people on the roof alone and about 88 on the bus altogether. On and on down the valley we went weaving our laborious way sometimes at river level and then slowly winding upwards again. We felt like an overloaded bee staggering up a vertical wall.

Three hours later we arrived at Balikot where we had to change buses. Disentangling ourselves and our possessions we clutched everything and heaved ourselves, stiff and cramped, out of the bus. The urge to find a "loo" fairly insistent before, had become a dire necessity. It was not to be. Our mini bus awaited and was leaving immediately. We had all of ten seconds to stretch and have a breather before we squashed ourselves back into place. Not a murmur had Duncan made. He had had nothing but a packet of biscuits, and a bottle. With no room to move for hour after hour, we wondered just how much he could take. It seemed any amount. He loved it.

Into the gathering darkness we went. The view was dismal in the extreme since the rain had not let up all day. Some amongst us dozed as best they could. We still had to decide what to do when we got to Abbottabad. Should we make for a friend's house there or to keep moving and try to get home? Duncan decided us. We would make for Islamabad.

In the bus station we disgorged ourselves and searched for the bus to 'Pindi. It was ten o'clock at night and we had no idea whether we had missed the last one. A bus was to hand. Leaping over the oily puddles we sought its shelter and found a square of benches at the back. We understood why the occupants already on the bus had left it vacant. There was a leak in the roof above our heads and puddles on the floor. Our cheerful grins froze.

Duncan was fed a cocktail of baby milk and "7up" in his bottle, which had the effect of high octane fuel. Far from inducing sleep he bounced about happily on whoever would have him.

Three hours later we arrived in Rawalpindi bus station. Weary but triumphant, we only had a short ride home. We had been twelve hours on the road. We had survived the bus ride. We had seen people and a life close to, hitherto denied us. We had been accepted and ignored by the country folk as if we had come from the villages ourselves. It was a unique experience that we would not have missed for anything.

The end of the story came with Colin next day when he finally returned with Razak.

The common calamity had brought all the drivers of the vehicles stranded at the rockslip together...in our Land Rover. The locals climbed in unable to believe their luck as the whisky bottle was brought out. Attempts had been made to clear the tons of rock by trying to knock a hole for dynamite with a crowbar and mallet. Into it was stuffed some dynamite, but five inches was scarcely sufficient. When the dust cleared twelve inches had been blown off the rock. Two hundred tons remained exactly where it was. After the third attempt, a German who had been watching decided to take matters into his own hands. Using a Unimog truck equipped with an air compressor drill he made three holes three feet deep and packed them with dynamite. A mighty explosion rent the air which had the crowds scattering for cover. It had worked. In no time the bulldozers had pushed the fragmented rocks over the ledge, and the way was clear. The German got no thanks for his labours. A flying rock had cut the compressor air line. It was lucky the first attempt had been successful or it would have been back to the hammer and chisel again!

The rockslip had been caused by marble being quarried up on that particular hill. Their explosions had loosened the earth... and the rain had done the rest.

Trying to deliver a letter

I arrive at the office of the local newspaper, *The Muslim*, to deliver a letter. Inside a bored girl sits at a typewriter

ME	Excuse me, is Mrs Hyatt here please?
HER	She is in the office three doors down the road.
ME	Thank you.

I go outside and walk down the pavement. Three doors down, a doorway leads to some officess upstairs. I decide to try there. Inside is a bare stone passage, dirty doorwayss and nothing that resembles a newspaper office. A toothless man runs after me up the stairs.

TOOTHLESS	What do you want please?
ME	I am looking for Mrs Hyatt, is she here?
TOOTHLESS	In there please (pointing to an office where two men sit in a bare stone cell dwarfed by two enormous typewriters)
ME	Is Mrs Hyatt here please?
THEM	Grunt...Silence, then they turn to look at each other and then at me...from top to toe.
ME	Does anyone speak English here?
ONE	No English please (big grin).

Toothless comes in.

TOOTHLESS	Please Mrs Hyatt is in Karachi. Her office is in there.

He points to a grimy doorway with a broken lock. I go to have a look. It is not her office. It is an empty kitchen. Vacant stares follow me as I thunder down the steps back to *The Muslim* office.

ME	Is this *The Muslim* office?
HER	No. *The Muslim* office upstairs.

Footprints of the Past

Colin's father had been posted to Peshawar. It was here that Michael, Colin's brother, had been born in 1927. We thought that if we searched the records of St John's Church we might be able to find the register of his baptism.

Without much difficulty we were able to locate the priest in charge who agreed to escort us to the church. Sixty years is a long time and many registers would have been used since 1927. Somehow we would have to unearth all the ancient records from the deep recesses of the vestry.... 1960...1940..back we would have to go. More and more dusty books were lifted from shelves and cupboards. Blowing dust off a battered old leather register, its edges frayed and worn, we finally found it. Excitedly Michael and Colin turned the pages. There it was! Michael Victor Geoffrey Francis. Mother, Kathleen, father Captain J A I Watts Royal Corps of Signals. Baptised on November 14th 1927. There was the proof! Michael's parents had brought him as a baby to that church. It brought those far off days very close.

Thanking the priest for his help, Colin and Michael wandered around the church trying to reconstruct the family scene of those far off days. What a shame that their parents, now long dead, could not share this return to the past.

The register had provided some other interesting information. We now knew where they had lived. We must go and see if we could find their house. Artillery Road was but a short distance away. Slowly we walked along the length of it. Using a bit of guess work since there were few numbers, we finally thought that we had found No. 42.

Set back among the trees and shrubs in a garden rather overgrown, was a sandy coloured bungalow typical of the Raj era. A verandah ran around the outside, its tiny windows set high in the thick walls. We opened the gate and walked up the path, the sun dappling the flowerbeds. Who lived there now? Would they mind if we looked around? We were spotted as we approached the door, a dog barked and a man came out to see who it was. When told of the reason for our visit he could not have been more helpful. He was very happy to show us around.

To keep the house cool, bamboo screens had been hung around the verandah and across the doorways. Inside, the rooms were dark and sparsely furnished. Fans were suspended from the high ceilings. The tiny windows provided little light or air. In midsummer the houses must have been very stuffy and airless. Mosquito nets hung over the beds and oil lamps were used at night. Conditions in the kitchen were very primitive. Cooking was done on kerosene cookers and there was no running hot water. Keeping cool and clean must have been a full-time job. It was little wonder that there was so much sickness and infant mortality in 1927. We guessed that little had changed since those days. Perhaps in England in isolated areas in the 1920s conditions would not have been too dissimilar. The owner of the house gave Michael a walking stick as a memento and instructions to return another day.

There was one more duty to perform, and that was that we should make the pilgrimage to Ranchi near Calcutta, to find Colin's mother's grave.

Our daughter Kay was born on her grandmother's birthday and had been named after her. It was appropriate that she should accompany us to India, so we planned to go when she came out from England to stay with us.

Aware of the splendid trains that crossed India we decided to go by rail to Ranchi. We flew from Islamabad to Delhi and it was there that we would join the train. Colin had booked sleepers for the three of us since the journey was to take thirty six hours.

We joined the seething mob of passengers on the platform of Delhi station. Families squatted down on the dirty ground among the refuse and the rubbish, waiting with patient resignation for the train to come in.

When our train finally arrived, Colin checked the names pinned on the carriage doors. To his dismay only two places had been allocated! Furious, Colin went off to the station master's office to complain and to demand that we should be given another compartment. It was hopeless. The train was already packed. Colin appealed to the guard for help who just shrugged his shoulders and took no further notice of us. We were going to have to take it or leave it.

We stared at each other. The prospect was appalling. Far from being the comfortable air-conditioned cabin that we had expected, the carriage that the three of us would have to sit, eat and sleep in for the next day and a half was a two bunked cell with peeling paint on walls that were painted dingy green. All it possessed were two hard, filthy-dirty torn rexine covered bunks. The walls and the floor were thick with dirt. There were rusty bars across the windows. A hole in the roof had let the rain in and puddles had formed in the floor. With only two bunks we would have to sleep in a shift system.

Bags and bundles were heaved aboard along the length of the train. Men, women and children clambered in after them. Curious dark eyes peered in at us as we stowed our gear and slumped down on our hard seats. The whistle blew and slowly the train pulled out of the station.

We left the depressing confines of back street Delhi and we were soon out into the countryside. We passed little villages made of mud huts with the most basic amenities. Oxen were ploughing the fields, while women in brightly coloured saris drew water from the wells. Huge wader birds with heavy black bills stood on one leg in the water meadows.

Hours later we finally stopped at a station. Thankfully we got out to stretch our legs. "Char wallahs" carrying thermoses of tea yelled for custom while pie vendors and samosa sellers stretched out hands into the windows hoping for a sale. Grubby urchins pleaded for backsheesh. We could not understand why a large crowd gathered outside our window, until we realised that they were staring at Kay's blue eyes! We bought some bananas and some tea and then retreated back into our cell. The tea was wonderful and we revived somewhat. We decided that we must avoid using the loo on the train. It was revolting beyond description.

Twenty nine hours to go! It was getting dark. A steward asked us what we wanted for dinner. Dinner? Was there a restaurant car? The man shook his head. Where on earth would it come from we wondered?

Outside the countryside was lush and green, bullocks sat submerged in pools of water beside more huge water birds. We sweated gently, warm air blew through the rusty bars as we hurtled through the heartland of India. We felt, looked and were filthy. The wooden seats were fiendishly uncomfortable so we stood for periods of time propping ourselves up against the dirty walls.

There was no water to wash in. The only hope of cleaning ourselves was with the flannels that I had brought soaked in eau de cologne. I was waiting until much later before bringing those out!

The door slammed open and three packets were shoved in. It was our supper! Wrapped in newspaper something vaguely resembling an omelette sat tired and cold on a paper plate. Starving but prepared to eat anything we fell on them, burning our mouths on tiny pieces of chilli that we had mistaken for tomato! Soon it was dark and the dim light overhead made it impossible to read. In need of some mental stimulation Kay and I made up limericks to pass the time. Those and other pathetic renderings kept us amused until we could delay going to bed no longer. Kay curled up on the top bunk with all the luggage and Colin and I slept head to toe on the bottom bunk. Somehow we dozed off.

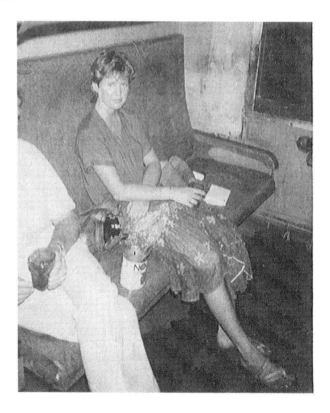

Kay on the train to Ranchi

We were woken every time the train stopped at a station. Rubbing hips and elbows bruised from the rocking, (there were no blankets), we peered out of the window to watch the crowds who shuffled on or off the train. Mosquitoes blew in the window and began to bite. Kay had the first suspicions of an upset stomach, so she was forced to visit the unspeakable loo. We changed bunks so that she could be near the door. We had been on the train for 13 hours. There were another 23 to go!

With the first signs of dawn, thankfully the long night came to an end. We had left the flat meadows behind. Here there were hills and hummocks and forests. We had absolutely no idea where we were. It was raining heavily, one leak dripped onto us on the bunk which Colin tried to catch with an old tin. We tried to clean ourselves up with my flannels as best we could. Calls of "Chai" had us sitting up eagerly. Handed in at the door in a thermos by a black hand, (we never did see who delivered our supplies), we voted it the best tea we had ever tasted! Hot and sweet it was wonderful.

There were 13 hours to go. Propped up on our bench trying to read or gaze out of the window the interminable day went on. We were heartily sick of the dreary journey. The hours were broken by a tray of curry and chappatis pushed through the door. There were no spoons or forks to eat with so we had to use our dirty fingers. Bottled water followed and thankfully we washed ourselves with it. I looked at myself in a mirror and could hardly recognise the hag from Holloway prison that stared back!

Seven hours to go. Weary and dirty beyond belief we were in a state of listless apathy. Our dingy cabin 7ft by 3ft had become a prison. We were bored by the countryside and too weary to read. We all felt dehydrated as we had had very little to drink and we had been sweating all the time. The end could not come quickly enough.

At 1.00 am as we lay miserably uncomfortable on our second night, the slowing down of the train and signs of habitation told us that at last, at very long last, we were approaching Ranchi. Stiff and exhausted, we hardly had the strength to drag ourselves and our baggage out of the train. Pushing and shoving we followed the crowds up the stairs. We had no idea where we were going to stay the night. Outside the station it was pouring with rain, dull yellow lamps giving everything a Dickensian look.

Across the road we saw some rickshaws.

"Let's get him to find us a hotel," said Colin.

He went across to the driver, spoke to him and then climbed into the back to await us. He waved us over. The driver had ideas of his own. No sooner had Colin jumped in, when the driver set off pedalling at a frantic speed down the road. The sides of the cab flapped about like a demented bat as it leapt and bounced in and out of the black puddles.

"Follow me!" yelled Colin as he vanished around a corner.

Thinking that we had lost him for ever, we jumped into the nearest cab and pointed frantically after him. It was pure luck that we were taken to the same hotel.

The hotel had a room the three of us could share on the top floor. There was a bed each! What luxury! One after the other we flung our filthy clothes off and disappeared in a sea of bubbles in a bathroom that had no bath or shower, but it did have a big bucket, a baler and an abundance of hot water! Utterly exhausted but clean at last we fell into bed.

We had got there! Perhaps in not quite the conditions that we had expected and maybe not in a manner that we would wish to repeat, but it had given us an unforgettable opportunity to see and experience a bit of typical India.

Ranchi in daylight presented an equally depressing sight. The heavy rain in the night had turned the roads into quagmires. As we emerged after breakfast to start our search for the cemetery, we had to paddle along, inches deep in sloppy mud to find a rickshaw. In stark contrast to the grubby surroundings, troops of children in spotless white shirts, blue skirts and ties were on their way to school. Combed and brushed and very smart they could have been transplanted from a typical English school.

We had no means of knowing where the military camp had been in the war or where Colin's parents had lived. Time was very limited and with little in Ranchi to attract us, we decided to spend all our time looking for the cemetery.

Our first port of call was the English church, St Paul's Cathedral. The church stood, large, grey, blackened and bleak as we approached. It was typical of the churches built by the British in the last century. As we peered inside, we saw a young man who, when told of our mission sent us around to see the Bishop. He lived close by in a spacious bungalow surrounded by trees. Steps led up to a verandah set about with pot plants and rattan furniture.

The Bishop and his family made us very welcome and his charming wife went off to order tea for us. They were very interested in our story and where we came from. We were told that there was a thriving Christian Community in Ranchi and that many visitors came to share their fellowship. The parish was very large and the Bishop had to travel great distances. He had never been to England. He told us that there were two cemeteries in Ranchi, the military and the civilian ones. We would have to see the priest in charge who would have the burial details.

The priest lived in a bungalow down a long lane surrounded by banana trees. Isolated and semi-derelict it looked a lonely place to live. A few chickens scratched around the threadbare grass. It had started to rain again and water dripped off the roof. We knocked on the door, hardly expecting to find anybody at home. We were unprepared for the very strange-looking man who came to the door. Was he the priest? If so he had gone very native! He had a brown blanket slung over his shoulder over a tee shirt, and he wore chapplis on his feet. It was not his appearance that we noticed so much as his face. He had frightening eyes that stared at us unblinking, a fixed grin that showed a few blackened teeth, and he had slicked-back black hair. He was very sinister. I thought that he must be a priest of a very different kind! We told him the reason for our visit and he went off to look for the register of Kay's death. Sure enough he found it! We peered over his shoulder at the inscription written at the time of her death.

"Kathleen Watts, aged 41 wife of Lt Colonel J A I Watts 15th Signal Company. March 9th 1943. Cause of death Cholera". There it was! The date of her death was significant too! We had been married on March 9th! We thanked him very much.

We left our strange host who seemed to live in a world of his own. He had not been back to England for years. One felt the magic of the East had affected him and his less than arduous duties had allowed him to go native.

Before we left he gave us a plan of the cemetery so we could locate the grave.

We found the cemetery of the Church of Northern India without difficulty. A muddy track led to the entrance and a gate, beyond which the graves lay on flat open ground. In the pouring rain the cemetery presented a dreary picture. It was obvious that little was done in the way of maintenance. It was a sea of weeds and long grass. Slowly we picked our way over the wet grass looking for the grave. Without the plan we would never have found it. That a grave was there was hardly apparent under the long grass. We stood there and stared at it. It seemed unbelievable that in this muddy and unattractive place Colin's mother lay.

Dearly beloved by all who knew her, she had been a devoted wife and mother of her three sons. For Colin's father Kay's death had been an appalling loss and he had been devastated when she had been struck by the dreaded cholera. In 1943 one presumes that there had been no Christian cremation for cholera victims, and to bring her body home to England in wartime would have been impossible. Cubby would have had no alternative but to leave her behind to be buried where she had died.

Colin's mother's grave, Ranchi

We wished that we could have told her of the family that had grown up through the years, of her fourteen grandchildren and twenty-one great grandchildren. A total family now of forty-three. It was a tragedy that none of us had had the pleasure of meeting her. It was distressing that she had been laid to rest so far from home but we were comforted that we had been privileged to be in a position to represent her large family and pay her our respects.

We could not put flowers on her grave since there were no flower shops in Ranchi. We could not cut the grass over her grave. All we were able to bring away with us were photographs, and some grasses that we picked from the top of her grave. These we would press and take back to England for Kay's sister.

We had fulfilled the pledge made when we arrived in Pakistan that we would make the pilgrimage to Ranchi and to find and visit Kay's grave.

Our time in Pakistan had brought the past vividly to life as we had tiptoed into the past and visited some of the places known to Colin's parents. It had been no wonder that they had chosen to make their life in India. In our own short experience of the people of Pakistan we had fallen under the same spell. For the rest of our lives we would never forget the kindness, courtesy and charm of all those that we had met. We could never forget the mountains and the valleys and places of unbelievable beauty. I will always treasure that opportunity for me, one military memsahib, to pay my respects to my mother-in-law who had also been a military memsahib!

A Country of Contrasts

Of high mountains and flat plains
Of arctic cold and searing heat.
Of Emperors' palaces and mudded huts,
Ancient cultures left behind
By traders and invaders
Who came in peace or stayed to fight.
We share a mutual respect.
Charming and courteous,
Unassuming, curious
Evasive and persuasive,
Vociferous and volatile,
Industrious and idle,
Genial and generous
We go with a debt we cannot repay.
A shalwared people restrained by a faith
Imposed by men.
Shrouded bangled Begums
Who silently sit among cushions.
Your hardened sisters in the fields
Have little rest from toil and sun
Welcome! sparkling ladies who broke free!
Who smile and talk of many things!
Dressed like birds of paradise
We fall beneath your spell
Those of us who stay awhile
And learn to love this Pakistan.

Killing Silently : American Sniper Chris Kyle's Lethal Moments

Sniper of Vietnam War : The Shots of Marine Sniper Chuck Mawhinney, In a Fly

500+ Kills - Sniper Ivan Sidorenko : WWII Hero of the Soviet Union

Deadly Sniper Duels - The War Story of Controversial Duel Between The Soviet Sniper Expert Vasily Zaitsev And The Mysterious Top Nazi Sniper in WW2

Titan Fails

Titan Fails - Vietnam War : How & Why America Lost the Vietnam War

War Classics In a Fly

Battle of the Atlantic, in a Fly : Long 2,075 days of War in World War 2

Battle of Midway, WWII Naval Battle in a Fly : Captivating Read on the Motives, Strategies, Tactics and the Winning Events of the Decisive World War II Battle

Battle of Okinawa, in a Fly : A Chilling Epitome on the Bloodiest Battle in Pacific Theater of World War 2

D-DAY, in A Fly : Deceptive Operation Bodyguard, Gruesome Battle of Normandy and the Aftermath

American Civil War, in a Fly

World War II Military Operations